EIGHT
GREAT WAYS
TO
HONOR
YOUR
WIFE

DAVID CHADWICK

HARVEST HOUSE PUBLISHERS
EUGENE, OREGON

Cover by Writely Designed

EIGHT GREAT WAYS is a series trademark of The Hawkins Children's LLC. Harvest House Publishers, Inc., is the exclusive licensee of the trademark EIGHT GREAT WAYS.

EIGHT GREAT WAYS™ TO HONOR YOUR WIFE

Copyright © 2016 David Chadwick
Published by Harvest House Publishers
Eugene, Oregon 97402
www.harvesthousepublishers.com

Library of Congress Cataloging-in-Publication Data
Chadwick, David, 1949-
Eight great ways to honor your wife / David Chadwick.
      pages cm.—(Eight great ways)
ISBN 978-0-7369-6725-9 (pbk.)
ISBN 978-0-7369-6726-6 (eBook)
1. Husbands—Religious life. 2. Marriage—Religious aspects—Christianity I. Title.
BV4528.3.C38 2016
248.8'425—dc23

2015030504

Printed in the United States of America

16 17 18 19 20 21 22 23 24 / VP-CD / 10 9 8 7 6 5 4 3 2 1

To my mom and dad, Helen and Howard Chadwick,
who honored each other and the Lord they loved and served until
their last breath. I'm glad you're together in heaven.
I look forward to seeing you again!

To my beloved wife Marilynn, who has honored me with her life,
faith, and love. I hope my life has honored you as well. I honor,
value, treasure, and esteem you beyond mere words.

To my three children, Bethany, David, and Michael,
who have honored me mostly by choosing to love and serve my
Lord and Savior, Jesus Christ. Your lives and choices have
honored me well. May your children honor you too.

CONTENTS

What Does It Mean to Honor Your Wife? 7

1. Trust Her Gut 11

2. Be a Man of God 23

3. Encourage Her Gifts 39

4. Respect Her Opinion 57

5. Ask This Question Often 77

6. Share Your Heart 95

7. Be a Guardian and Gardener 113

8. Use Words Wisely 131

   Epilogue: Honor in Action 151

   A Husband's Honor Code 161

   Study Questions 163

   Notes 181

What Does It Mean to Honor Your Wife?

The word *honor* has become missing in action in the English vocabulary. Oh yes, sadly, we sometimes hear about an "honor killing." Most often, that's when a child rejects a certain faith tradition. The father feels he must kill the child for the sake of honor in his home. There is also "honor among thieves." They still seem to hold the word *honor* in high esteem. The Boy Scouts still begin their pledge with "On my honor, I will do my duty." Some schools still emphasize an honor code.

But in reality, the word *honor* isn't much talked about today.

The importance of the word *honor* has not been abated in the Bible. Children are to honor their mothers and fathers (Exodus 20:12). Rulers in the government (Romans 13:7) and the elders who preach, teach, and lead the church are to receive a double honor (1 Timothy 5:17). Widows who serve others (1 Timothy 5:3) and friends who labor for us (Philippians 2:29) should also be given honor because of their personal importance in our lives. Christians are to honor one another, even above self (Romans 12:10). When Christians behave with honor, it should draw spiritual skeptics toward faith in God (1 Peter 2:12).

And honor is supposed to be given by a husband to his wife (1 Peter 3:7). He is to honor her as one with enormous value. In this verse,

Peter says that a wife is to be treated as a "weaker vessel." I don't think this idea expresses inferiority at all. I believe Peter used this phrase to describe a fine, delicate piece of pottery, like porcelain. The wife is supposed to be like a priceless vase in her husband's hand. He is to treat her with great care and gentle esteem, tenderly showing to her the enormous value she holds in his life.

In the New Testament, the Greek word translated "honor" is *timen*. It can refer to a prize, esteem, value, recognition, or respect. The opposite of honor is shame. To dishonor something or someone means we are ashamed of it or the person.

To honor something or someone means it or the person is very valuable; indeed, a treasure—something or someone about which or whom you're not ashamed. When you feel shame, you feel worthless. Shame is the antonym of honor. So when we honor God, we are saying he is infinitely more valuable and prized than anything on earth and therefore worthy of our worship.

What does the Bible mean when it tells us to honor our wives? Let me put it in a way our culture can understand. She is a trophy—a person dearly prized. She is the husband's ultimate, permanent trophy bride! When you look at your wife, you can't believe she is a part of your life. You consider it a high privilege to be married to her. You want others to know the value she has in your life. You are honored she is your wife.

What would happen in our culture if we stopped looking at our wives as being someone placed on our arms to make us look good? What would happen if we truly understood what biblical honor means and desired to value our wives by recognizing them as prized, permanent trophies?

When we truly show honor as we should, we will treat our wives as a priceless treasure—a person of immense value and worth. As King Solomon wrote, "A man's greatest treasure is his wife" (Proverbs 18:22).

This book is about eight great ways to honor your wife. My wife, Marilynn, has written an accompanying book entitled *Eight Great Ways to Honor Your Husband*. We both are trying to recapture the significance and importance of this word *honor*—especially in the marriage relationship between a husband and a wife.

We both believe God gives his original design for marriage in the creation narrative (Genesis 1–2). In Genesis 2:20, Eve (*isha* in the Hebrew) is taken from Adam's side (*ish* in the Hebrew). These two were once one. When separated, the goal is for them to come back together as two equal and complementary partners. Only these two different people can cleave and weave their lives together.

In Genesis 2:24, God gave his order and goal for marriage: one man, one woman, in a committed, complementary, permanent, heterosexual, monogamous relationship. At the end of this verse, God gave his intended desire for these two complementary people coming together: oneness. He wanted the two to become one flesh.

He wants my love for Marilynn and Marilynn's love for me to swim through our veins like fish in the sea.

At the end of all marriage days, God wanted a man and a woman to be inextricably one. His design was the strange, mysterious, profound intermixture of two hearts and souls. I am to become one with Marilynn. She is to become one with me. At the end of our married days he wants our fingers tightly squeezed together, expressing the mingling of our lives together. That's God's will in marriage. That's why he created it.

You will see this theme of oneness in marriage interwoven throughout this book. Honoring one another as husband and wife is one of the major ways this goal from God happens.

Let's be very clear: Honor is not the end goal of marriage. But it *is* very important in marriage. Marilynn and I would not have written these two books if we didn't think so. But it's an aid. It's a means to the end. The goal is two becoming one. Learning to honor one another unequivocally helps this occur.

Isn't there something within you as a husband that resonates a desire to be permanently one with your bride? Doesn't your heart and soul long to know this reality? Don't you yearn to imagine yourself at the end of your married days with your fingers still interlocked with your beloved in marriage, joyfully sharing together a lifetime of collective memories?

Most couples do. And I believe God himself is the one who placed this longing within the hearts of those whom he has called to marry.

But it doesn't happen overnight. It's a lifetime of tiny, imperceptibly different threads sewn together through a husband and wife's different choices. But at the end, nothing should be able to separate a man and woman who have become one—especially as they choose to honor one another.

Let me give you one final thought. These eight great ways to honor your wife may paint a picture of me that's not entirely accurate. Yes, I have practiced them throughout our marriage. But some were learned by what I didn't do correctly. Moreover, like most all husbands, I've regrettably stepped on Marilynn's toes too many times. My human hubris hasn't allowed me immediately to apologize, as I should have. I think Marilynn would say the same thing.

But we both keep trying. We both keep moving toward one another. We both are committed to practicing honor to the end, cheerfully embracing marriage as God intended it to be.

That's because we want oneness more than anything else in our marriage.

We are now almost 40 years strong. We love each other deeply. We regularly practice these eight great ways to honor each other in our marriage. We are more in love today than we were when we married. Our love grows by the day. We are permanently bound together. Our oneness is increasing by the day, month, and year.

Marilynn is indeed my lifelong, imminently treasured trophy bride!

I hope these eight great ways to honor your wife will help you feel the same way about your wife.

And mostly, help you and your wife become one.

1

Trust Her Gut

I WISH I'D BEEN smarter in this area. If so, I could have avoided a lot of pain. I stupidly ignored this reality. If I could redo one major part of Marilynn's and my marital life together it would be this one. I'd trust her gut more. I'd honor her intuition.

It's happened not once, but on multiple occasions. Marilynn sensed something was wrong. Her spiritual antenna was high. It was receiving strong signals. She sensed an unknown something. There was an inward, environmental stimulus without any accompanying reason. It caused extreme tightness and discomfort in her stomach area.

She couldn't explain why she undeniably sensed what she did, but she did. She just knew something wasn't right. Something was out of whack. Something bad was about to happen. Her gut was twisted and nervous. There was a foreboding something on the horizon. And she was saying to me that I just needed to trust her gut.

Too often I ignored her suggestions and plowed ahead with what I needed to do and thought was best. I'd give a polite nod. Or sometimes I'd argue back, saying she didn't understand the full picture. Or sometimes I was totally dismissive and I'd say she simply needed to trust me. Looking back, I often ignored her instincts to my own eventual chagrin and demise.

Fortunately, she's seldom poured on guilt by saying, "I told you so." She's been gracious when I've later acknowledged her wisdom and my folly. But on many occasions I've gone to her and simply said, "You were right. I was wrong. I'm sorry. I should have listened to you." If there is one positive thing that's come from these excruciating experiences, it's that I learned great humility.

Again, I wish I'd been smarter. In this area, hindsight truly is 20/20.

Some people call it women's intuition. Others refer to it as a gut instinct. I'm not exactly sure of the appropriate term. But I know it's true. Women have something inwardly that men don't have. They receive insights on situations men tend to ignore.

A Natural Gift

What is intuition? It's the unusual ability to acquire knowledge without inference or the actual use of reason. There's little scientific research and evidence on the subject. But it does exist.

Women in general, and my wife in particular, have a natural gift. There *is* something to intuition. Perhaps it's what Pilate's wife felt when she warned him to have nothing to do with Jesus (Matthew 27:19). From my experience, it is something men generally don't possess in the same way women do. Yes, men do have gut instincts. They are oftentimes useful and insightful. But they don't have it like women. It's a special gift. There's no comparison.

Some women object to this statement. They feel it's misogynistic. Others try to explain it away through female stereotyping. Some say it's because of biological differences between males and females. Others say it is caused by the different ways genders communicate. Others say it's a learned behavior, deeply rooted in living through different life experiences. Some suggest it's a way women have learned how to deal with and manipulate men through the ages. Still others suggest it is caused by estrogen affecting the brain's subcortical functions. Huh? This last one is beyond me.

Again, there's not much scientific data. We really don't know why it works. And I'll have to leave the potential scientific causes of women's intuition to people more learned than I. All I know is it does work. I've seen and experienced it on multiple occasions in my marriage and with other women. Of that I'm certain.

And I think it should be especially operational in a marriage relationship. If the goal of marriage is two different people becoming one, it makes sense that when the wife feels something is awry about a situation that her husband is walking through, then her gut instinct is what's best for both of them in their lives.

That means when Marilynn is feeling something, she's feeling it for me! If we are one flesh, spiritually connected and intermixed, that means God may be using her as a sensitive vessel to speak to me, warning me of a potential problem. Therefore, I need to listen to her. I need to trust her gut.

Through the years, I've learned that Marilynn is on my side. Like God, she is for me (Romans 8:31). She wants the best for me. She wants me to succeed. She desires for me not to step into stuff that will hinder me. If this is so, I must trust her gut.

Sometimes Marilynn has insights into people. Other times it's insights into situations. Still other times it involves both. Often she can't explain why she's feeling what she's feeling. She's just feeling it. It's like a red warning light blinking brightly on a car's dashboard. It's to be taken seriously and acted on immediately. It's alerting the driver to a problem in the engine. If not taken care of soon, the engine is imperiled and could break down.

That's a good analogy of what a wife's gut instinct does for a husband. It's an alarm bell that needs to be heeded.

But let me restate my premise. I believe women's intuition is real. I've personally experienced it in my relationship with Marilynn. There are many, many times I wish I'd trusted her gut and listened to her intuition about certain issues occurring in my life. I'd have been wiser and able to avoid much pain.

Life Illustrations

There are two general areas in which Marilynn's intuition has come into play and I have tended to ignore her. The first relates to our kids' sports activities. The second is in the area of church staff.

First, there's her intuition with regard to our kids' participation in sports. Being a former athlete myself, I invested heavily in their sports success. I knew what sports had done for me. I'd learned invaluable life lessons. Sports are a microcosm of life as a whole. They had taught me discipline, hard work, personal responsibility, and teamwork. I learned how to win with joy and lose with grace.

I wanted my kids to learn what I'd learned through sports. So I became deeply involved. Plus, I really enjoyed the time we were able to share together—much like what my dad and I were able to experience.

As our kids all became increasingly involved with their sports, at different times, I'd have a blind spot when it came to coaches. Outside of parents, coaches are some of the most potent influences in kids' lives. They are teachers and their classroom is the court, field, or diamond. They should be positive role models to whom kids look for life lessons. They should emulate the values of parents, reinforcing what is being taught at home.

Yet on several occasions, Marilynn sensed a disconnection between our values and those evident in one of our kid's coaches. She would flinch when an angry word was hastily spoken to a child. Or she would see a permissive attitude toward what the coach would watch publicly at the movies or on television at home. Or she would notice pieces of literature in their home that we'd never permit in our own. Or she'd be concerned about whether the coach really believed in our kid's giftedness and not give fair opportunities we knew he or she needed or deserved.

Marilynn would feel keenly uncomfortable as she observed these kinds of things. Frequently she would wait weeks before she'd say anything to me. She didn't want to overreact. But the gut's discomfort persisted and grew.

Finally, she would voice her concerns to me. She would wait for the right moment, and speak respectfully to me. She would make it perfectly clear that her greatest concern was first for our kids. But she was also concerned that I or the church could be negatively impacted as well.

I'd love to tell you I was a godly man who immediately listened and acted. I wish I could tell you that I rightly trusted her gut. But too often, I didn't. I tended to quickly wave away her concerns, most often hiding behind my knowledge that I understood sports better than she.

Marilynn would occasionally remind me that this had nothing to do with my sports acumen, but about her care for the kids and me. That didn't help either. I still didn't listen.

Later, after finally concluding she was correct, I'd have to painfully and carefully extricate us from the problem. There's a leadership adage that says, "It's easier to get in than out." How true it is! It's much easier to start something than get out of it when it's a mess. If only I had heeded her counsel earlier, I could have avoided a lot of the pain of the mess.

The other area is with church staff. Marilynn would sense long before I that there was a potential problem. Sometimes she would notice incompetence. Or she would hear someone using foul language for effect. Or she would feel disrespect from someone toward me. Or she would notice people who thought faithfully following a secular business model was more important than nurturing the spiritual life of the church. Or she would sense people forming relationships behind-the-scenes that later expressed themselves in power plays against me.

She would warn me. She felt that was her obligation as my life partner.

But I wouldn't listen. As happened with the coaches, I'd assume I knew better. I was living in the arena of the church every day. I was the expert. She wasn't. I knew better than she what was really going on. Surely people weren't that devious or incompetent. Surely in ministry circles people didn't live out personal agendas for their own glory. Surely church staff wouldn't do these kinds of things.

But I was naïve. I was too trusting. I wanted to believe the best in people. I wouldn't acknowledge human hubris. It was difficult for me to believe that people had agendas—especially those who said they were faithful followers of Jesus.

Looking back, I have some painful memories. It's hard to admit to blind spots and places where you're not self-aware. But successful leaders need to do it. I've needed to do it. It's not optional.

I've repeatedly asked myself why I didn't listen to Marilynn. I've wondered why I didn't honor her by trusting her gut.

A Painful Lesson

After having gone through these two painful trials, and trying to become more self-aware, I've asked myself these pertinent questions: "Why didn't I initially trust her gut? What made me become defensive and dismissive when confronted with her concerns?"

And I can come up with only one answer. It wasn't pretty. The Lord revealed to me an ugly side of my fallen nature. Bottom line, I didn't trust her gut because I wanted something better for my glory. I wanted something greater for me than I wanted my wife's input.

With sports, I wanted my kids' success. I overlooked rather obvious character flaws and problems with coaches because I wanted them to succeed too badly. Their success would make me look good. Their success was a positive reflection on me. Marilynn's input, therefore, needed to be secondary to what I desired for my own glory. Ouch.

With the church, I wanted its success more than I wanted Marilynn's input. The staff consisted of people I was hoping would help the church grow. Some of these people were younger, hipper, and seemingly more relevant. They brought an organizational business model that had proven successful in other churches. They could help the church reach out to younger people and become even more successful than it already was.

That's idolatry. It's using people for my glory. Ouch.

Do you see the consistent pattern? I wanted something more than Marilynn's gut instinct.

It's been a painful lesson to learn. But I think I've learned it. To honor my wife, I need to trust her gut. If we are one, as God intended all married couples to be, the Lord will speak to me through my wife, who is a part of me. When Marilynn speaks to me from her gut, it's for my good. And I may well be listening to the voice of God for me when she's speaking from her intuition.

I honor Marilynn when I trust her gut.

A Word to Wives

I find it interesting that there is not much scientific data to explain the phenomenon of a woman's intuition. Personally, I think it's a special "something" God has given to women from the beginning. It's a spiritual warning system God has formed within them.

And I also think a wife's intuitive ability to hear from God is directly connected to her prayer life. Her gut instinct is docked in heaven's harbor; it resides in eternity's halls. And as she seeks God, his heart is made known to her. Perhaps her prayer life opens a special door to receive the spiritual gift of discernment (1 Corinthians 12:10).

I think that's the case with Marilynn. Almost every morning, I see her sitting on the couch with her Bible open and her "chubby" book before her. What is her "chubby" book? That's a nickname she's given to the book in which she lists her prayer requests. On the pages, she lists every day of the week. Then, under each day of the week, she has people, places, and organizations for which she prays.

For example, you'll find me listed under Monday. Elsewhere, she has included other family members and friends. There are some missionaries listed in there. She fervently prays for each one. (For more information about this prayer strategy, please purchase Marilynn's first book, *Sometimes He Whispers, Sometimes He Roars.*) I know she seeks God daily. I know she wants the doing of his will to be the master passion of her life. I am certain her heart is connected to God's heart every morning.

Therefore, I can trust her gut. I can fully anticipate that her concerns to me about a situation may be from the heart of God through her to me.

If you're a wife who is reading this book, this means that if you want your husband's ear, God needs to have your heart. And the best way he can have your heart is through prayer.

Have you examined the depth of your prayer life recently? Seeking God daily will increase your gut instincts. It will enlarge your woman's intuition. It will increase your husband's desire to know what you have to say. It will encourage him to trust your gut.

Practical Suggestions for Husbands

There are some practical things we husbands can do to give our wives the best opportunity to speak to us and help us avoid stepping in stuff we shouldn't. Here they are.

First, set aside time regularly to be together and alone. This theme recurs over and over again throughout all the eight great ways to honor your wife. It's an essential. You can't hear your wife's gut unless you spend time together. You can't become one without time together.

Second, ask her opinion on issues in your life. Desire her complete honesty and perspective. If something doesn't make sense, ask again for clarification until it becomes clear. Pay special attention when she says, "I don't know why I feel this; I just do!" Or, "I've got this inner vibe that just won't go away. It keeps twisting my stomach into knots." That's probably her gut instinct in operation.

Third, consider all your motives as she shares her gut. Are you refusing to listen because you want something more? If so, you're entering dangerous waters. Beware! You are probably soon approaching a mostly hidden and destructive iceberg. And believe me when I say it's much easier to get in than out.

Finally, take action. If your wife is warning you about a person or situation that just doesn't "feel" right to her, at least pause. Examine carefully what she has noted. Even if it may embarrass you, you'll most likely need to back out. Even if the situation at the moment seems prosperous, you may find yourself needing to run in the opposite direction of the deal. Trust me—you'll be glad you did.

You may want to start keeping an "intuition journal." What is that? It's a journal listing all the times your wife's gut instinct told you about something and she was right. Then read that journal—repeatedly! As you observe the number of times her warnings were right, it'll cause you to pause and listen to her more in the future. My journal has many chapters, unfortunately.

Trust your wife's gut. Listen to her intuition. I've learned through the years that this is a badge of honor I gladly pin on Marilynn. It's a badge she actually wants to wear.

When I listen to my wife, I honor her. And it creates more oneness between us.

And the more I listen, the fewer problems I have in life.

That, within itself, is a very good reason to trust her gut.

STAYING STRONG PAST
THE HALFWAY POINT

What is a reward? It's receiving something for hard work and effort. It's a paycheck. It's recompense. It's something earned.

Did you know God offers rewards for faithfulness to his followers? When the Israelites were in captivity, God commanded them to be faithful in Babylon. He told them to marry, build homes, and work hard for the welfare of the capital city of Babylon while they lived there (Jeremiah 29:5-6). He had a plan for them, one filled with a future and a hope (Jeremiah 29:11). He promised that their faithfulness would eventually be rewarded when they returned to the Promised Land (Jeremiah 31:16).

Jesus promised eternal rewards for his followers. For example, he said that giving to the poor, done in secret and not seeking the applause and approval of people, would be seen and rewarded by his Father in heaven. He said the same thing was true for praying and fasting done in secret (Matthew 6:1-8, 16-18).

He also said that when someone gives a cup of cold water to people in need, they don't lose their reward in heaven (Mark 9:41). He said that when people suffer and are persecuted for following him, their reward in heaven is great (Matthew 5:11-12). He said that when he returns with the angels in all his heavenly glory, he will reward each person according to his works (Matthew 16:27).

Paul mirrors this same teaching. He said that all people will face a judgment of works (2 Corinthians 5:10). Therefore, no one should ever become weary of well-doing. At the proper time, he will reap a harvest of rewards (Galatians 6:9).

I should pause a moment and comment about the difference between eternal salvation and eternal rewards. Eternal salvation is not earned. It's a free gift from God through Jesus Christ (Ephesians 2:8-10). Any work we do is in response to the gift of salvation by grace through faith.

Yet our good works do reap a reward. This reward is directly connected to the choices we make here. More specifically, they are connected to good works. What we do here affects what happens to us in heaven.

Some of those rewards include ruling with Jesus in eternity (Matthew 24:45-47). We will judge with Jesus—especially over the demonic forces that have caused this world much pain (1 Corinthians 6:2-3). We will receive different crowns for our faithfulness to him here on earth—crowns we will immediately cast down at the feet of Jesus when we start worshiping him in heaven. We will realize anew that our ability to earn crowns here was only because of his grace (Revelation 4:10). Jesus alone is worthy of all praise.

But I'm convinced the greatest reward any one of us will receive for our faithfulness here on earth will be Jesus' simple statement "Well done, good and faithful servant" (Matthew 25:21). His hearty approval for our faithfulness is the best of all rewards.

Husband, you are told to honor your wife (1 Peter 3:7). A reward for doing so is that your prayers will not be hindered. Perhaps there are many husbands who have not received the earthly reward of answered prayers because they've not learned how to honor their wives. Heaven alone will reveal this possible reality.

But I also wonder how many husbands ever consider the possible connection between honoring their wives and eternal rewards. Isn't honoring our wives a biblical command? Isn't it also a part of earthly faithfulness? Could it be that Jesus' "Well done" is attached to how well we husbands honor our wives here on earth? Shouldn't we desire to be faithful to our wives till death do us part?

I am convinced the two are connected.

Since this is most assuredly true, may I warn you about a trap that may prevent long-term faithfulness? I've sadly witnessed the effects of this trap in multiple marriages through the years.

It's the trap of the halfway point. For example, when you are halfway through a project, you become tired and lose your focus to the point of wanting to give up. You just don't know if you can keep going. Runners feel it when they are at the halfway point of a marathon. Nehemiah felt it from his workers when they were halfway through the building of the wall around Jerusalem (Nehemiah 4:10).

I'd suggest the enemy of our soul knows this reality. He attacks perniciously at the halfway point in our marriages. He adroitly knows how tired our souls are. He knows how vulnerable we are to quitting, giving up, and chucking our marriages and families and wanting to find something new.

One night, Marilynn and I were watching a television special about a famous World War II bomber called the *Memphis Belle*. The documentary chronicled the plane's 25 combat missions in World War II.

There was a little-known fact that caught my attention while watching the program. When groups of these bombers reached their destination, they would be greeted by puffs of black clouds all around them. These clouds were exploding artillery shells fired from the ground, spitting shrapnel in every direction, trying to hit and down the plane before the bombs were dropped. Seldom, however, did this artillery fire stop the planes from dropping their bombs.

It wasn't until after the bombs were dropped that the real fighting began. This marked the halfway point in the mission, during which there would be an eerie lull as the planes turned around to return home. Suddenly, tiny black specks appeared in the sky. They became larger by the second. These were the enemy's fighter pilots. They began the bitter battle to down as many of the bombers as possible before their return home.

It was during those several minutes at the halfway point in the mission that the bombers were most vulnerable to the enemy. With their machine guns blaring, they resisted the smaller, more agile fighter planes as best they could. Their main hope was that their large numbers and near-perfect formation would help prevent a large number of casualties.

On the *Memphis Belle*'s last bombing expedition, 36 planes took off. Only 29 returned, the *Memphis Belle* being one of the fortunate ones.

Again, when were they most vulnerable? It was at the halfway point—just like it is with runners. Just like it was with the people who were rebuilding the walls of Jerusalem with Nehemiah.

That can happen to us as well at the halfway point in our marriages. It's when familiarity and ennui set in with our wives. It's when our jobs demand the most from us. It's when bills mount and kids demand more time and money from us. It's when the enemy attacks most ferociously, trying in every way possible to divide the marriage.

One major way for us to defeat the enemy is to steadfastly refuse to give up and instead, continue choosing to honor our wives. We continue to value them no matter what the timing or circumstances of our marriages. We keep working through whatever issues there may be. We keep moving toward oneness. We believe that if God brought us together, nothing can tear us apart.

Why do we want our marriages to last till death parts us? Yes, we want to honor our vows. We want our children to witness success for the sake of their marriages. We want our wives to be honored. We want our prayers to be answered. We want other earthly rewards that may accompany our faithfulness. We yearn for heavenly rewards and crowns at the judgment of our works.

But above all else, we desire to hear Jesus say, "Well done, good and faithful servant" when we finally appear before him. Those few words, spoken from his heart to ours, are the revered reward that can help us to persevere through the halfway blahs and the evil one's wiles. Those few words are what help inspire us to conquer any trial we face.

Husband, honor your wife. It's the right thing to do. It makes you one with her. It makes you faithful. And it especially makes you ready to hear Jesus say, "Well done, good and faithful servant."

Don't you desperately desire to hear those words?

2

Be a Man of God

CHILDREN DIDN'T COME EASILY to Marilynn and me. We had to wait eight long, arduous years before our daughter was finally born. She was a miracle from God. Marilynn had severe endometriosis. By supernatural intervention, God healed her and we conceived. We were daily overwhelmed with gratitude for this gift.

Our first son came more than three years later. We were astounded that God gave us two children from a barren womb. We were then completely surprised by God when our second son arrived almost five years later.

Before our children were born, Marilynn and I made a decision that we wanted their names to reflect our hoped-for character qualities they'd one day possess. We spent hours trying to think and pray through possible names for them.

Our daughter Bethany's name means "house of rest." We sensed that she'd be gregarious and love people. When people would come to know her, they'd find in her a welcoming, gracious, loving rest for their weary souls. Her middle name—*Brame*—is Marilynn's maiden name. Bethany is connected to all the great people of faith in Marilynn's heritage.

This was true of our sons' names as well. We wanted them to be men of God who relentlessly loved and pursued their wives. We desired their marriages to be permanent and filled with enormous joy. We wanted their wives to experience them as honorable men. Therefore, we chose names that we felt would rightly indicate what a man of God should look like.

We named our firstborn son David Banner. The name *David* means beloved. King David's name may well have expressed his beloved character more than an actual name. After all, the Bible describes him as a man after God's own heart (Acts 13:22). We wanted our son to be tender of heart toward all who would cross his path in life—especially his wife.

The *Banner* part of his name has a two-part origin. First, it was from my family. My mother's side of the family had a history of Methodist circuit-riding pastors. Several of them had *Banner* in their names. They must have been tough, grizzled, veteran men of God to travel from town to town, week after week, to preach and teach God's Word.

Second, *Banner* is one of the biblical names for God. In Exodus 17:15, we read these words: "Moses built an altar and called the name of it, The LORD Is My Banner." The altar was a memorial built in tribute to God's deliverance of the Jews over the Amalekites. The picture here of God is one of a strong, mighty warrior, dressed for battle, one who ferociously fights our battles for us.

When you put together our first son's name, *David Banner,* you have the picture of a beloved warrior. You have a man who is tender and tough. That was our hope for our son. That's the kind of man of God we wanted him to be.

Surprise!

Marilynn and I were quite satisfied to have two beautiful children— a boy and a girl. After years of infertility, we couldn't have been more thankful to God. We knew both were gracious gifts from him.

Five years after David was born, Marilynn came downstairs while I was watching a sporting event (what else is new?). She had a peaceful but serious expression on her face.

"I have something I need to tell you," she said. I muted the sound on the television—ready to listen, but still wanting to catch glimpses of the action on the screen.

"Sure, what's up?" I asked.

"Well," she stammered, "I just took a pregnancy test, and it proved positive."

Gulp. Say what? We were both a bit older in life. We were thankful for the two children we had. Marilynn had always believed there would be one more, even when most thought it was implausible, perhaps even impossible.

Here was my first question back to her: "What's the accuracy rate of the test?" I really didn't know what else to say.

"Ninety-six percent," she responded. She not only anticipated my question, but she had wanted to know herself.

"When can you take another one?" I immediately retorted.

"In an hour," she quietly responded. We both simply nodded. She went back upstairs. I restored the sound on the television as my mind considered the future consequences of this unexpected development.

Marilynn came back downstairs an hour later. She sat and looked into my eyes. This time I turned off the game.

"It says I'm pregnant," she said calmly.

Still not knowing exactly what to say, I responded, "What's the accuracy rate for the second test?"

She knew. She had read the label. "Ninety-eight percent."

I gently approached her and kissed her on the cheek and squeezed her hand. I told her how much I loved her. Then I got up, walked to the door, and said, "I need to go out for a while. I'm not sure exactly where I'm going. But I will be back. Promise." She nodded. She understood what was happening in my heart.

I then got into my car and started driving, not knowing my destination. I passed a movie theater and decided to go watch a movie. There was a 10:15 showing of *A Clear and Present Danger* starring Harrison Ford. It was an appropriate title for what I was feeling at that moment! I purchased a ticket and went in. I think I was the only person there.

I don't remember much about the movie (I later watched it on television—actually a pretty good movie!). During the two hours I was there, my mind churned over facts: *Okay, I'm this old. And when I'm this age, the child will be this old. And I'll need to make sure I work this long to get him or her through college. I need to keep physically fit, eat well, and exercise.* My mind tried to discern all the possible future life situations.

Finally, my mind became weary. I just sighed and prayed, "Lord, you are the author of all life. Obviously, you chose to give Marilynn and me another child. It must be your will. Therefore, I give you this child. I trust you with this child. You will give me whatever I may need to be a good father to this child. You will provide. You promised to do so. It's all in your hands."

I arrived home well after midnight. I crawled into bed, hugged Marilynn, and again told her I loved her. She asked, "Are you all right?" I assured her I was. I really was. In fact, I was becoming increasingly excited about what God wanted for this child.

When we learned we would have another boy, Marilynn and I went through the same exercise we did with David Banner. We wanted to name him with our hopes for who he'd become as a mature man of God, someone who would honor his wife throughout his life.

Marilynn was the one who came up with the name *Michael Hunt*. She explained that the name *Michael* means "Who is like God?" It's a rhetorical question that serves as a clear statement that no one is like God. But it also refers to a true worshiper of God, someone who humbly knows that God is God and he is not. Also, Michael is the eventual conqueror of Satan at the second coming of Jesus (Revelation 12:7-8).

The *Hunt* part of Michael's name comes from Marilynn's side of the family. She has traced her lineage back to the Hunt family that fought in the Revolutionary War in Massachusetts. Many of them were brave militia who heroically and tenaciously fought the British for our nation's independence.

Can you now see who we wanted Michael Hunt to become? We wanted him to be a humble worshiper of God as seen in the definition of the name *Michael.* But we also desired him to be a tough fighter for truth and justice as the archangel was when he conquered Satan and as the Hunts were when they courageously fought for American freedom from the British in the Revolutionary War.

Our dream for David Banner was a godly man who would be tough and tender, a beloved warrior. For Michael, we hoped for a godly man who is humble and heroic, loving and serving God all his life. By balancing the two traits represented in the meaning of their first and middle names, we saw both our sons being great men of God.

And they would learn to honor their wives. Ultimately, they would accomplish what God wills for all marriages: They'd become truly one with their brides.

After decades of listening to women share their hearts, I'm convinced that they desire their husbands to be true men of God. They want their character to secure these same balances. When they see these qualities present in their husbands' lives, they feel honored, prized, and valued. They are drawn toward their husbands. And the result is oneness.

Regardless our names, we husbands would be wise to see if these types of qualities exist in our lives.

DESIRABLE QUALITIES FOR EVERY MAN

Based on my sons' names and other biblical insights, here are several two-word character qualities that I believe God would love for all men to exhibit—character qualities all women would love for their husbands to have.

Husband, ask yourself if you'd want these character qualities to describe you.

Heroic Warrior

Dudley Do-Right was a cartoon character. Regularly, he bumbled and fumbled his way toward heroic success. Often after he'd delivered the damsel in distress, she would coyly sigh and say to him, "My hero."

Some might suggest that the saved damsel's praise of Dudley's heroism is misogynistic drivel. I don't think so. I think most women yearn for their husbands to be heroes. They want to believe their husbands are willing to sacrificially die for them as Jesus did for the church (Ephesians 5:25).

That's true love—not some syrupy, ever-changing feeling, but the willingness to die so the other can live. Jesus said there is no greater love than that of laying down one's life for another (John 15:13). This type of self-effacing, sacrificial heroism enhances the wife's respect toward her husband. And respect is what a man longs for from his wife (Ephesians 5:33).

Similarly, she yearns to see his heroism take strong stands. She wants to see him as a mighty, ferocious warrior, dressed for battle, someone doggedly fighting for truth, justice, goodness, fairness, and righteousness.

These strong stands may be reflected in a stand for all life—in and outside the womb. Or perhaps it's a commitment against sex trafficking. Or maybe it's being an outspoken advocate for racial equality. Or perhaps it's a dogged stand for justice for the disenfranchised and marginalized in our world. Maybe it's working to ensure all have clean water and food. Or perhaps it's a desire to reach the world for Christ.

Wives hunger for husbands who are heroes. These kinds of strong convictions honor our wives. They solidify respect in their hearts.

I remember when Marilynn and I received an invitation to visit a church in Beirut, Lebanon. At the time, the ISIS crisis in Syria was great. This church had a ministry to many of the almost four million displaced refugees from Syria. Many of the refugees were living in tents a few miles from the Syrian border, hopelessly alone and destitute. The church members wanted to take us to a tent village just a few miles from where much of the fighting was going on so we could get a first-hand picture of what was happening.

There was reason to pause whether to accept this invitation. There appeared to be a certain amount of danger. ISIS was not far away.

Finally, I felt the Lord's nudge to go. I sensed that inner whisper saying to me, "If you don't go, who will? I am calling you both to go." I told Marilynn we needed to go. She hesitatingly consented. When I told the congregation we were going, there was some trepidation. But I simply asked, "If not us, who?"

We went. It was one of the most powerful experiences we've ever had in our ministry. We saw Lebanese Christians acting as the hands, feet, and mouth of Jesus to hundreds of displaced Syrian refugees. They were tirelessly serving the people group that years earlier had been persecuting them! One Lebanese man shared how the Syrians were responsible for his father's death. Now he was visiting displaced Syrian refugees in the tent village, sharing with them the love of Jesus.

Not only did we visit the tent village, we also were able to sit down with a Muslim woman and her eight children and talk to them about what had happened to them.

One night, she and her family were peacefully sleeping. Suddenly a rocket shrieked through the silence of the night and ripped through her home. She lost her husband and one child. She desperately grabbed her remaining children, a few belongings, and ran toward the nearby Lebanese border. She entered the tent village. There was no other place to go. She had experienced extraordinarily heart-rending tragedies. Yet she was smiling. She continued to care for her children. She even served us tea. She chose to continue to live in hope that one day she could return to her homeland.

Later, after leaving the tent village and entering Beirut, Marilynn and I continued to walk with these Lebanese Christians as they cared for similarly displaced refugees in the center of the city. Thousands now lived there. The vast majority of them were Muslims.

We visited one family on a rooftop in downtown Beirut. The Syrian civil war had also caused them to flee their home. The husband sought work every day to provide food for his family—most often without success. His eight-year-old daughter was a brown-eyed beauty, looking strikingly like my own daughter at the same age. Her sole desire was to attend school and be educated. We made a commitment to try and help her do so. It's my pleasure to say she is now in school.

During a worship service in the middle of the week, Marilynn and I preached the gospel of grace to hundreds of Muslims, mostly women. We laid hands on and prayed for the sick. We saw food and clothes distributed to the needy.

The next Sunday, I preached at the church. One of the Muslim women for whom I'd prayed earlier in the week excitedly approached me. Through an interpreter, she told me that after I'd prayed for her, God had healed her. She wanted to know more about Jesus. I bowed my head in humble thanksgiving to God for using me in this way.

While in Lebanon, we never felt any danger, though we were told it was surreptitiously there. Nevertheless, we went. I sensed God's voice, and I obeyed. Marilynn followed, believing that God was leading us both through me.

Upon our return, I wrote an article for the *Charlotte Observer* about the needs of displaced Syrian refugees. I've tried to become a warrior for their situation. Forest Hill Church has begun a partnership with our church friends in Beirut. Several mission trips have happened. Forest Hill's ministry there continues.

And, at the end of the trip, Marilynn took my arm, snuggled close, and said, "Thank you for going. I really respect you for that. It was heroic."

Was it heroic? I don't know. But Marilynn thought so. She thought I was a heroic warrior. And that's what is important to me—that she thinks so. And that we grow closer together as one.

Humble Worshiper

I believe that humility is primarily rooted in the worship of God. The two most important biblical terms to consider when it comes to worshiping God are "creation" and "new creation." Let's explore both these terms in relation to humility.

First, there is "creation." According to Genesis 1:1, God created the heavens and the earth. The Hebrew word translated "creation" is *bara*. It tells us nothing existed before creation. The Latin term *creatio ex nihilo* is often used to describe the Genesis account, in which we are told creation came from nothing. God merely spoke a few words, and all creation occurred. He didn't create the world from something else. He created it from nothing else.

How does this relate to humility? Consider this: How is it possible for us to be proud if God made everything from nothing? Everything in this world, including all humanity, came from God's sovereign hand. In recognizing this truth, we should all cry out as the psalmist did, "Who am I that you are mindful of me?" (see Psalm 8:4).

Every inhalation of our next breath, every bite of food, every piece of clothing, every friend we cherish, every possession we have—everything—comes from the God who created everything from nothing. Our only posture in life should be one of humility. Every human is a beneficiary of grace.

Second, there is "new creation." The Bible teaches that all of us inherited a selfish nature at the moment of conception. Some find the doctrine detestable. Personally, I don't. I believe it for two reasons. First, the Bible clearly teaches it. Second, it's the best explanation for all the evil and suffering in the world. Every day the evening news convincingly proves the doctrine of original sin.

Because of this selfish condition, we are hopelessly separated from our Creator. Our puny works can't ever make us righteous before his perfect holiness. It's impossible.

Therefore, since we can't cross over to God by our works of righteousness, God must come to us. He put on human flesh in the form of Jesus. He lived the perfect life we could not live because of our sin problem. He died in our place on the cross, taking our sins upon himself, something he didn't deserve. From him we can receive the forgiveness of our sins and eternal life, something we don't deserve. We can have new hearts. We can become new creations. The old has passed away and the new has come (2 Corinthians 5:17).

How is this free gift of forgiveness given to us? It's received by grace, not works (Ephesians 2:8-9). If by works, we'd boast about it. But we can't. It's a grace gift. That means God did the entire work. It's similar to *bara* and *creation ex nihilo*. Our dead, wicked hearts have now been made alive through Jesus Christ.

Do you see how the truth about the "new creation" causes humility? If my heart is dead in sin and trespasses (Ephesians 2:1), God and God alone is the one who made it alive. If I had nothing to do with my old, dead heart coming to life, and if my new life is totally a gift from a gracious Father in heaven through Jesus, what do I have to be proud about? The answer is nothing—absolutely nothing!

Let's now take this idea a step further: Humility is rooted in the worship of the God from whom *all* blessings flow—my creation and my new creation. Worship is identifying with the name *Michael* and asking, "Who is like God?" The answer is obvious: no one. God is God. I'm not God. And most of my problems come when I get those two things confused!

Worship becomes a joy for the husband who truly understands "creation" and "new creation." He hungers to worship with his wife. He hopes his children will see him as a true worshiper of the one true God, a worshiper filled with humility.

Thanksgiving constantly fills his heart. He is daily and eternally grateful for everything God has graciously given. He is able to praise God in all things, knowing there is a plan and purpose in everything, even difficult times (1 Thessalonians 5:18).

A wife who knows that her husband is a humble, thankful worshiper can trust him to lead wisely. She knows he has humbly submitted himself to a Boss who leads him. She knows he has her and the family's best interests at heart. She knows humility is akin to honor. A humble husband who honors God will also want to honor his wife.

Marilynn and I met on a blind date. She was a bit hesitant to go out with a seminary student. I had hesitations too. She had just graduated from the University of Georgia and was a sorority girl. Not knowing much about each other, we both tried to check each other out before the date, calling mutual friends and acquaintances to give us any insight as to whether we should even have the date, much less enjoy it.

One such friend Marilynn called about me, fortunately, gave her a positive report. She said I really loved God and wanted to serve him. But the one thing that Marilynn has always remembered about her comments about me was this one: "He's amazingly humble for what he's accomplished." Later she told me that was the one statement that made her open to accepting a blind date. She wanted a humble worshiper. Now nearly 40 years later, I'm glad she did!

A Forgiven Forgiver

A husband honors his wife when he humbly and heroically takes the initiative to pursue his wife and practice forgiveness. The ability to forgive flows from a heart that is heroic and humble. It is the result of a man who worships God and fights for his family.

Ruth Bell Graham, Billy's wife, once said that the best marriages are made up of two great forgivers. She's correct! Two very different people, living in a permanent marriage relationship, will at times step on each other's toes. We hurt each other—sometimes willfully, sometimes not, sometimes a little, sometimes a lot.

When the husband is the offender, he needs to pursue his wife and say, "I'm sorry. Please forgive me." He needs to swallow his pride. He should approach her in profound humility.

Why? For Christians, a willingness to forgive flows primarily from God's forgiveness of us through Jesus Christ. Jesus taught his disciples to pray, "Forgive us our debts, as we also have forgiven our debtors" (Matthew 6:12). Paul echoed this teaching that we are to forgive one another as Christ has forgiven us (Ephesians 4:32; Colossians 3:13). God has forgiven us a billion-dollar debt for our sins through Jesus' death on the cross. Therefore, in comparison, we are to forgive those who owe us a trifling, smaller debt. A worshiper follows the instructions of the one he worships!

But there's a second reason to practice forgiveness, and it's rooted in humility. If everything is a gift from God, especially our eternal salvation, how can we not say, "I'm sorry; please forgive me" to the person we love most in the world? Not to do so expresses pure pride. It's awful arrogance. It's haughty hubris. It reveals that we actually worship self, not God.

A husband who won't forgive doesn't honor his wife.

Bridled Power

In Matthew 11:28-29, Jesus said, "Come to me, all who labor and are heavy laden, and I will give you rest. Take my yoke upon you, and learn from me, for I am gentle and lowly in heart, and you will find rest for your souls."

Jesus described himself as "gentle and lowly in heart." The Greek word used here is *praus*. Literally, it can be translated as "bridled power."

It's the only adjective Jesus ever used to describe himself. It describes a person who has learned to bridle his great gifts and power. It describes the King of the universe bridling his eternal power by humbly taking on human flesh to die as a servant for humanity (Philippians 2:5-11).

When I wanted to give Forest Hill Church a visual image of what the word *praus* means, I brought a horse on the stage in the sanctuary. The congregation laughed in shock as the horse came out. The owner then placed a bridle on the horse's mouth and guided him across the stage. The horse dutifully obeyed the owner's nudges with the bridle.

That's when I said, "Folks, that horse could easily overpower anyone in this room. But because there's a bridle over him, and the owner is guiding him, the horse is using his full gifts in a controlled manner. That's the meaning of the word *praus*. It means bridled power. It's what should happen when we all are under the power of the one who created us. That's humility."

Shouldn't *praus,* bridled power, be a word used to describe a husband who is a true man of God? Wouldn't heroic humility be God's desire for all husbands? Wouldn't a forgiven forgiver strive to be a blessing to his wife? Wouldn't being a worshipping warrior make you a well-balanced husband?

What About You?

I'm convinced these character traits are what most wives desire from their husbands. When carried out, they honor the wife. And that, in turn, increases the wife's respect for her husband. The end result is a greater oneness between them.

Husband, what about you? Do your character qualities reveal that you are a true man of God? Do they honor your wife?

AN HONOR BENEFIT: LOOKING LIKE ONE ANOTHER

People have joked about how those who love their pets start to look like them as the years go by. Various photos have been posted online to prove the point. Some pairings are extremely humorous. Other pairings show striking similarities. When you have some time, type in "Photos of pets that look like owners" and get a howl yourself!

But the same can be said about husbands and wives who really love each other and have been married for a long time. In fact, in a benchmark study in 1987, University of Michigan psychologist Robert Zajonc assiduously analyzed photos of couples when they were newlyweds and then 25 years later. It became obvious to him that the longer that husbands and wives were married, the more they started looking like one another.

To make sure his findings weren't mere speculation, Zajonc asked groups of people to look at the different pictures as well to determine who was married to whom. He randomly mixed up the photos of those who had been married for 25 years or more and asked people to guess marriage partners simply by examining their facial resemblances. This was the sole criterion by which they were to be matched.

Remarkably, in practically every case, individuals who had been married for 25-plus years were matched with their spouse. There was a convergence of similar facial appearances. Astoundingly, in some cases, the group concluded that some couples could probably pass for one another in a dimly lit room.

Different explanations have been offered by supposed experts to understand and explain this fascinating phenomenon.

One suggestion is that women chase after men who look like their fathers. Therefore, there is a natural, genetic similarity that will exist from the beginning of the relationship because of a woman's Daddy desire. That resemblance will naturally and inevitably increase as the years go by because there was commonality in appearance from day one.

Others suggest what's called "assertive mating." This idea is contrary to the popular opinion that opposites attract in marriage, and states that genetic commonalities draw a man and woman together. You are drawn to people like yourself. Some suggest this is narcissism lived out in marital choices. If true, over the years it is only natural you'd start to resemble each other more and more.

Still others believe that when you live with a person for a long time, you start to mimic them. You subconsciously copy the one you love, making this a "monkey see/monkey do" explanation for facial similarities in marriage. When he/she smiles, the other mimics it because the other is admired so much. The same is true with a frown. Over time, his/her smile or frown marks become yours.

These are interesting suggestions. But the truth is, no one knows why couples start to resemble one another after years together in marriage. No one definitive study has sufficiently answered the question.

But few can deny that it's true.

I have a suggestion to explain this phenomenon—at least in the case of Christian couples. If true, it is totally unrelated to all the other suggestions. Here it is: Perhaps it's an inward reality expressing itself outwardly on the couple's faces. Perhaps it's the oneness of their hearts that causes their outward appearances to eventually become similar as well.

In Ephesians 5:31, Paul quoted Genesis 2:24—the most profound verse about marriage in the Bible. It talks about how two opposite yet complementary forces come together in marriage and become one flesh. Then in verse 32, Paul said this union is a divine, profound mystery, like Christ becoming one with his church.

God sent Jesus into the world to change us from the inside out. Mere legalism can never change a heart. That's an outside-in life change. It doesn't work. No heart has ever been changed by trying to obey laws.

The only way the heart can be transformed is by the powerful, selfless love of Jesus. When we receive him inside our hearts, our dead, self-centered hearts are united with his alive, gracious one. Our hearts then begin to take on the character qualities of Jesus. Over time, changed from the inside out, we are gradually conformed to the image of Jesus (Romans 8:29).

When this new birth by the power of the Holy Spirit happens inside a man and woman's hearts, and they are subsequently drawn together in marriage, they are mysteriously enjoined. That's how they are brought together. That's how they become one. The life of Jesus inside each of them infiltrates the other. An old gospel song describes it as the Jesus in me loving the Jesus in you.

This inexpressible, mysterious, joyous oneness melts two distinctive hearts together. Over the years, this oneness is deepened. A husband and wife grow increasingly closer and closer. As years give way to decades, their hearts become even more inextricably connected.

The bond becomes so strong that they can never be separated.

That's what Jesus meant when he said that a man and a woman enjoined by God's Spirit are no longer two but one flesh. And what God has joined together, no flesh-and-blood person should ever separate (Matthew 19:6).

Therefore, the best way to safeguard a marriage against divorce is for the husband and wife to continually develop and deepen the spiritual bond between them. When this happens, nothing and no one can ever break that bond. What God has joined together, no person can ever separate. It's impossible. Their lives are one.

If this is true—and I'm certain it is—here's my question: If the decades cause hearts to become increasingly one, doesn't it make sense to think this inward reality must eventually express itself with an outward resemblance? Like a joke that touches the heart and forces a smile, wouldn't the inward, mutually shared love between a Christian man and a woman force similar outward expressions?

Paul said this inward oneness is a mystery. Mysteries can't be explained by science. But this mystery of shared resemblances does seem to have some obvious scientific verification.

Which makes me very happy. For those who have looked at me, and also looked at Marilynn, they tell me that I can only hope and pray this is true and that I'll look more and more like her as the years go by.

I do hope and pray it! I know I got the better end of the deal. I'm the lucky one. I know I married well above my pay grade. Daily I stand in amazement that she said yes when I asked her to marry me.

She's that beautiful in my eyes. For being married to her, and all the many other blessings I've known by being married to her, I'm eternally grateful.

It's yet another reason I need to continually honor my beloved. When I do, inward oneness grows. And I'll increasingly start looking like her.

Wouldn't that be great news?

3

Encourage Her Gifts

WHEN I FIRST MET Marilynn and learned of her accomplishments, I was absolutely amazed. She possessed numerous gifts. Her resume was eye-popping. Her future appeared extremely bright for whatever field of endeavor she chose.

Academically, at the University of Georgia, she graduated second in her class with almost a 4.0 in journalism and international communications. She was a semifinalist for the prestigious Rhodes Scholarship. Her professors and peers voted her the outstanding woman on the University of Georgia campus her senior year. She was well-respected by all.

After graduation, Southern Bell recruited her as one of six women to join their corporation. This was during the time when businesses were specifically targeting gifted young women to create more equality in the workplace. They assured her she was on the fast track to corporate, executive, and financial success. She excitedly accepted their offer and began her work.

Soon thereafter, we met on a blind date. I know—for most of you who have seen her and me, you think she must have been blind! But, by God's grace, we fell in love with each other quickly and thoroughly.

Three months after we met, we were engaged. Then six months after that, we were married. Yes, I broke every rule I give to engaged couples. "Give it the test of time," I counsel. "Overcome all doubts by spending time with one another. That's the safest way to go."

But we just knew. Now, almost 40 years later, we are glad we got married!

After the wedding, Marilynn and I spent our first year together in Houston, Texas. I was doing an internship at a church as a part of my in-sequence Doctor of Ministry degree. Marilynn approached Southern Bell and told them of the move. She said she wanted to spend that first year building a strong foundation for our marriage. And because she was still a relatively new Christian, she also knew she needed time to ground herself in the faith and understand the church.

Southern Bell knew they were losing a gem. They recognized Marilynn's extraordinary potential. Her overseers said they understood, but they also made it clear they wanted her back. They said that when she returned with me to Atlanta after my internship year, the job would still be available for her.

During that year in Houston, Marilynn's faith grew exponentially. She was truly my helper and strength when it came to forming relationships, ministry groups, and outreaches. It became increasingly apparent that her life's calling was not corporate America, but ministry.

When we returned to Atlanta for my final year of seminary, Marilynn calmly told Southern Bell that she didn't want the job. They were disappointed but said they understood. Instead, she accepted a job with the Southern Baptist Mission Board, helping to write articles for one of their magazines. It didn't pay much. She didn't care. She continued to grow in her faith. It was a sterling year of growing closer together.

We accepted the call to Forest Hill Church in 1980. For our first year in ministry, Marilynn told me she wanted to get our home secure and learn what it's like to be a preacher's wife. Fortunately, the wonderful people at Forest Hill never placed any expectations upon her. They simply wanted her to be her!

That's what she did. She was always by my side, as a gracious wife and helper. In those early years, when Forest Hill was small, we were everything from the youth leaders to pastoral counselors to Bible teachers to prayer leaders. We were involved in everything that went on in the church—mostly because we had to be.

Yet I knew that underneath her servant's heart laid a greatly gifted woman of God—gifted in ways I wasn't. I knew she had much to offer the world. She had already sacrificed much to follow me. Therefore, I wanted to encourage her gifts.

Encouraging Marilynn's gifts was all about releasing her God-given potential. As her husband, her life partner in marriage, I was in a better position than anyone else to make that happen.

Have you ever thought about that as well—that you as a husband are the one person who is most able to encourage your wife's gifts? God has gifted her in special ways—in fact, she's gifted in areas that you aren't. God brought you two together because he knew you could help bring the best out of each other.

Biblically, husbands are called to love their wives (Ephesians 5:25). In my opinion, one of the best ways you can demonstrate the love of Jesus to your wife is to help her launch her gifts.

Before I share about the ways you can do that, I'm going to share examples of ways I have come alongside Marilynn. My hope is these examples will inspire you toward encouraging your wife's gifts!

Encouraging Marilynn's Gifts

Her Academic Gifts

Marilynn loves to learn. One day, after a couple years of ministry at Forest Hill, she expressed a desire to grow in her learning. Children had not yet come. At that point, we didn't know how long God would keep us waiting before we had kids. I began to ask the Lord—and Marilynn—what we could do to address this love of learning.

The answer soon became clear to both of us. Why not go to the University of North Carolina-Charlotte and pursue a master's degree in counseling? She had the time and desire. It would help her in ministry.

Marilynn enrolled and was accepted. She loved her classes. She was engaged in helping many people from all different kinds of backgrounds. And she secured her master's degree.

I was thrilled to see her happy. She was thankful I'd helped her rediscover her love for learning. But we both knew another step needed to be taken.

Her Ministry Gifts

Marilynn wanted to use her degree to serve others. She was gifted academically, and she had a huge heart for helping people. What could she do?

We both sought the Lord for his will. The answer soon came. The more Marilynn studied about the prolife movement, the more she knew she had to get involved. She knew a child's DNA was formed forever at the moment of conception. She knew there was a heartbeat at 21 days. She knew pain could be felt within months of conception. Sonograms had opened a door for all to understand the facts about life in the womb.

With my encouragement, Marilynn took her gifts of compassion, care, and academic acumen and helped launch the Crisis Pregnancy Center in Charlotte. Without pay, she selflessly gave her time to counsel young women caught in the quagmire of problem pregnancies. Her master's degree gave her the necessary listening skills to help them.

It also gave her credibility with community leaders. I vividly remember her telling me about taking a US congressman on a tour of the facility. She carefully explained what they did and why. She gave him the facts about what happens at conception and in the womb. She shared how sonograms had become God's way of speaking undeniable truth. The facts were obvious. He entered the facility unsure about where he stood on abortion. He left decidedly prolife.

While she was there, who knows the numbers of lives she impacted—both inside and outside the womb? I'm honored to have encouraged her gifts in this small way.

Her Gifts as a Mom

Children finally did come, albeit not on our schedule. I was completely supportive when Marilynn decided to stop all work outside the home so she could devote herself entirely to our children. Every step of the way, she snuggled, stroked, and loved them. She was there for them.

Plus, she encouraged their gifts to be launched into the world. Together, we helped identify what our children loved to do and the ways in which they were gifted. They are all adults now, and each one has reached a level of success in their life. I'd attribute their success largely to Marilynn's involvement in their lives as a mom.

Her Speaking Gifts

When our youngest, Michael, entered elementary school, Marilynn had more time available. With that extra time came an exacerbated desire to get more active in ministry again. It was a part of how God had wired her.

Because Marilynn is articulate, I had her help me with my weekly radio program. On special occasions, she would speak for or with me for the weekend worship services. Listeners enjoyed her insights. I also encouraged her to explore other opportunities to speak, which she did.

For example, Marilynn helped develop a ministry at Forest Hill called Women Under Construction. It's an outreach to spiritual seekers. Forest Hill women are encouraged to bring their seeking friends to an event at the church. For more than 20 years, the event has grown exponentially. Marilynn speaks at this event and hosts other speakers as well.

Many women have come to a personal faith in Jesus Christ as Lord and Savior because of this ministry. Interestingly, these women would then bring their husbands and children to church, and they too would meet Jesus.

Coming on Staff

It was a natural next step. As the kids grew older, Marilynn took the opportunity to come on staff part-time. She had volunteered in many different capacities. An opportunity arose for her to come on staff. I urged her to take it.

Fortunately, she did. One of her key ministries is organizing churchwide prayer vigils several times a year. She helps people know how to pray for nations, the persecuted church, and the sick in our midst. In fact, Forest Hill's present outreach ministries in Burundi, India, and Lebanon can be directly traced to Marilynn's listening ear to God in prayer.

Encouraging Our Gifts Together

One of the best decisions we have ever made is to serve together. It has brought us much closer. It has increased our oneness like nothing else.

It began in the early 1990s with a trip to Ethiopia to visit some missions efforts Forest Hill was supporting. I was also asked to speak at a Bible conference there. We had never done a missions trip together, and we sensed God telling us to go.

What an experience! We visited places where missionaries had risked their lives to take the gospel. In one village, an elderly gentleman told us he had formerly been a witch doctor. Decades earlier, he received a vision that a white man (which the people in his village had never seen before) would come and show him a large black book. He was told to listen to him and accept his words from this book as true.

Later, a white man carrying a black book came. Remembering his dream, this witch doctor approached him and listened carefully to his words. He knew that what he was saying was true. His heart had already been prepared. He received Jesus as his Lord and Savior. The rest of the village soon followed. Today there is a huge, thriving church in this area.

And what happened at the Bible conference? More than 35,000 showed up. Marilynn and I were deeply moved because many of these people had walked an entire day from their villages to come and hear God's Word. Many had boom boxes planted on their shoulders to record every word I spoke.

That trip dramatically transformed our lives together. A passion for world missions was ignited within our hearts. Since then, we've gone to the Sudan, Ghana, Kenya, South Africa, and Burundi in the continent of Africa. We've traveled to Lebanon and India. We've also gone to Europe to visit and encourage pastors and people there who are trying to plant churches in dark, secularized regions.

Each trip causes our hearts to grow closer together. Using our gifts as a team has significantly aided us in becoming one—God's goal for all marriages.

ENCOURAGING YOUR WIFE'S GIFTS

So in what ways are you encouraging your wife to use her gifts? Most certainly she is more gifted than you are in some areas. Without a doubt she would love for you to come alongside her and help identify and encourage her areas of giftedness and help launch them into the world.

How can you help make this happen? Here are some suggestions. What follows is not an exhaustive list, but ideas I've learned with Marilynn.

Prayer

Make sure you begin with prayer. Set aside times to be alone without interruption. Your sole purpose is to seek God together so you can find out his will in the matter. It could be that he is calling your wife to something that is not yet known or revealed to either of you. Or it could be God will confirm something you've already suspected. But first, go to him together in prayer. Ask the Lord about his will for your wife. You may be surprised what he reveals.

Listen and Watch

As you spend time with your wife and probe how to launch her gifts, listen to her voice as she talks. What subjects cause her to lift her voice in excitement? Conversely, what subjects seem to suggest disinterest on her part? These are clues regarding her passions.

Watch her body language as well. What causes her body to twist and turn with excitement as she talks? As one of my friends said, "Watch what makes her bottom bounce off the seat when she speaks." This will give insight into what tantalizes her soul.

The excitement in your wife's voice and body language are often great clues about where you may encourage her to launch her gifts.

Others' Perspective

Get input from others who know your wife well, especially if they are more mature Christians. Where do they see her as being especially gifted? What could they see her doing that she'd really enjoy, that would help advance the kingdom of God? Often, other people can see things we husbands don't see.

Then go to close family members and close friends. Get their input. Ask what areas they think your wife is gifted in. What can they see her doing that only she can do?

Duty-Free Time

All of us have daily obligations and responsibilities. Often they are immutable. Sometimes they are drudgery. But they must be done. They are the tasks we alone can do. We do them because we have to.

But most of us have "duty-free time" as well. It's time in our daily or weekly schedules set apart to do whatever we may want.

Watch carefully what your wife loves to do with her duty-free time. How does she spend it? Does she want to read and study? Does she gravitate toward times of prayer and intimacy with God? Does she desire to spend time with the kids and help them achieve something? Does she love to journal or blog? Draw and do art? (My dad noted my mom's painting acumen after the kids left home and encouraged her to take lessons—which she did—and she became quite the artist.) Does she love to take photographs? Does she enjoy visiting the needy and homeless? Does she like cooking food to take to a neighbor or shut-in?

How your wife spends her duty-free time will give good clues on what makes her heart sing. Observe how she uses her time, and you may gain insight into knowing where to encourage her gifts to be used.

Alone Time

Someone once said that you can discern what your idols are by noting where your thoughts roam when you are idle, alone, or giving yourself permission not to think about anything in particular. It's when you are idle that you discover your idols! I think there's truth to this statement. Your mind won't stay idle forever. Eventually, it will wander to something.

Often, your thoughts go to what you love the most. During those moments, you can tell what's really important in your life. Encourage your wife to list the things she thinks about during her "idle" time. Maybe this will give you both clues about where she may want to launch her gifts.

Open Doors for Her

As your wife's gifts, passions, and desires start to surface, find people who can help open doors for her. Find ways to make things happen. Networking your wife with others and coming up with ideas that would help launch her gifts should be a supreme joy for you. You never know if one of your connections or resources may be able to help your wife launch her gifts.

Be Her Biggest Cheerleader

Once you have both identified some opportunities and doors have started to open, be your wife's biggest cheerleader. First Thessalonians 5:17 states that we are to encourage one another as followers of Jesus. Shouldn't that begin with our spouse? Shouldn't you greatly desire your beloved's success—even above your own? Proverbs 31:28 tells us that the husband of the Proverbs 31 woman praised his wife. He encouraged her.

Hebrews 12:1-2 says that we are surrounded by a cloud of witnesses who are cheering us on to the finish line of faith. Who are these witnesses? Maybe they are the angels. Perhaps they are the saints who have gone to heaven before us. I love to imagine my mom and dad cheering me on from heaven, encouraging me to finish my race of faith well.

Do you know why geese honk when they fly in a V-formation? Researchers have discovered that geese fly 73 percent farther when they fly together rather than alone. Each goose plays off the updraft of the geese ahead of him. This makes the work of flapping their wings easier. By contrast, the lead goose is taking on the brunt of the headwind. In fact, the wind is so strong that if he were to look back, his neck would snap. That's why the geese honk as they fly—they are telling the lead goose they are still behind him, staying in formation. With their encouragement, he is able to keep moving forward and not look back.

If the Proverbs 31 husband praised his wife, and if there's a cloud of witnesses in heaven encouraging us to finish the race well, and if geese need encouragement, shouldn't we husbands similarly be encouraging our wives toward their goals and dreams? Shouldn't we be the loudest voices, encouraging them to launch their gifts for God's glory?

After all, if we are truly one flesh, and oneness is the goal of all marriages, doesn't that mean Marilynn's success is my success as well? And that her joy is my joy? Her accomplishments are my accomplishments? As love increases between you and your wife, shouldn't you want her success even above your own?

On several occasions, Marilynn has thanked me that I'm not threatened by her gifts. Why should I be? I'm honored that this enormously gifted woman has chosen me to be her husband. In some ways, we are similarly gifted. In other ways, we are very different. Praise God for the differences! When we use our differences to build each other up, oneness is the result.

Therefore, I encourage and celebrate Marilynn's gifts being launched into the world.

Most followers of Jesus eventually learn that life is not about us. It's about giving and serving. It's about God's kingdom being advanced. That's what's most important. That should be the driving force behind a husband encouraging his wife to discover her gifts and launching them into the world.

Launch Similar Gifts Together

Here is one final point of advice: As you encourage our wife to discover her passions, try to find those areas in which you share similar giftedness. When you do, if possible, try to find ministry and service opportunities you can do together. These experiences will draw you closer like nothing else—just like the missions trips that Marilynn and I do together.

I pray you will encourage your wife to discover and use her unique gifts. I pray especially you'll be able to find mutual areas of giftedness through which you can serve together.

That will especially help to draw you closer together. And make you one.

"I WANT YOUR LIFE"

Marilynn and my daughter Bethany have always been close. Bethany is uniquely gifted in her own right. She is a friend magnet. I've never seen anyone who develops and nourishes relationships like she does. She is also athletic, artistic, and intelligent—like Marilynn!

One day when Bethany was a teenager, she and Marilynn were talking, enjoying their time together. Out of the blue, Bethany said, "You know, Mom, I want your life." Marilynn blushed and brushed the comment aside.

"No, Mom," Bethany insisted. "You don't get it. I really do want your life. I really do!" Then they began to talk about what Marilynn's life was like as a mom, pastor's wife, worker, author, speaker, missionary, one who serves the poor, etc.

Now, some 15 years later, guess what our Bethany is doing? She is married to Ryan, who has planted a church right outside of Charlotte, a ministry that's part of the Acts 29 network. At the time of this writing, they have three kids. Bethany is intimately involved with helping Ryan plant the church. She cares for the people inside and outside the church. And most importantly, she is caring for their children. Indeed, she is living Marilynn's life.

My prayer is that as Bethany's future seasons continue to unfold, Ryan will continue to encourage all her multiple gifts to be unearthed and used. It's what I've tried to do with my beloved Marilynn.

It's what every husband should do, as two become one.

CHANGED LIVES

From the first time we met, I have loved Marilynn's tender, compassionate heart—especially for the poor. She has ferociously fought for the underdog, the downtrodden, the marginalized, the disenfranchised, and the needy. She vehemently despises racism and bullying. And she loves for people to dream big dreams and overcome large obstacles for success.

For example, amidst strong objections and tensions, she helped usher the first African-American girl onto her high school cheerleading squad. She didn't care what others thought. She knew racial equality was God's will. It was the right thing to do.

When we pass a person on the street with physical limitations or ostensible poverty, she always desires to give him money. When I question her wisdom in doing so, pointing out that the person may not be what he seems, she shrugs and responds, "He will have to answer to God one day for lying. I won't. I obeyed the biblical mandate to care for the poor. My conscience is clear before my Lord."

Her desire to care for the needy motivated her to find out how she could help financially challenged teens become more upwardly mobile. After all her research, she discovered that $5000 annually, coupled with an involved mentor, is often what makes the difference between a teen getting into college or not.

Yes, grants were available to these teens. But Marilynn discovered that often these kids would fall a bit short financially and subsequently quit. Thus arose the need for the $5000. Often they couldn't navigate the confusing forms for enrollment and grant aid as well. Thus arose the need for a mentor.

To address this problem, Marilynn worked with friends who possessed a similar passion and formed a ministry called Seeds of Hope Scholars. They committed to finding teens who had dreams but were financially challenged as well.

Once identified, interviewed, and properly vetted, these teens were matched with a mentor and promised a $5000-a-year scholarship. The mentor and the money were committed throughout the four years of college. The end goal was graduation from college and the Seeds scholar's entrance into a career path consistent with the dream.

As I saw the Seeds scholar program unfold, I was amazed to see teens with dreams going to college and entering the work force. Lives were being dramatically changed.

I encouraged Marilynn to pursue this work and tried to help her in every way possible—especially networking her with influential people for fundraising purposes. Before our eyes, teens with no future became teens filled with hope. Their dreams became reality.

Examples abound.

Shona stole cars as a teen. Her future faced a dead end. Her life crossed with Marilynn's, and they became friends. Shona was bright, articulate, and motivated. Marilynn asked her what her dream was. Surprisingly, she shared that she wanted to become a doctor—especially in underserved areas.

She needed a financial boost and received a financial grant as a Seeds scholar. She relentlessly pursued her dream.

Today, Shona is indeed a doctor serving, as you guessed it, in underserved areas. She is caring for people who are largely in despair. God is using her mind and hands to heal their broken bodies.

Quentin was ten years old when he found a broken-down piano on the side of the road. It awakened a musical dream in his heart. With his mom's permission, he rolled the piano into the garage. She said he could keep the piano in the garage, but he couldn't bring it into the house. That would never happen.

After he repaired the piano, Quentin taught himself how to play it by ear. As the years passed by, he became more and more proficient and skilled. He started playing and singing in his church's worship band. His deep, rich, resonate baritone voice reminded some people of Barry White in a Christian context.

His story was discovered and chronicled on the front page of the *Charlotte Observer*. Many in Charlotte were moved by this young man's persevering pursuit of his musical dream.

Interestingly, the church where Quentin was playing was a church that Forest Hill had come alongside, some years earlier, and helped build a new worship facility. We enjoyed a close, rich relationship with this inner-city church and often shared life and worship together.

I showed the story in the *Observer* to Marilynn and encouraged her to contact Quentin. She did, and a meaningful friendship between them formed quickly.

Eventually, Quentin became a Seeds scholar. After high school, he was accepted into a noted music program at a well-known university. He graduated, and is now leading, teaching, and writing music in a church. Marilynn and he remain good friends, communicating together often. He sees Marilynn like a member of his family.

Isaiah's story was also shared via the *Charlotte Observer*. He lost his mother at an early age. His dad worked hard to support him and his siblings. They didn't have much. But his father taught all the children about the need for personal responsibility and hard work.

Isaiah had a dream he wanted to pursue. He had been successful academically in high school. He wanted to graduate from college and be successful in life and in the business world as well. He didn't want mediocrity, but to use his gifts to excel in extraordinary ways. All that held him back was limited financial resources.

Marilynn contacted Isaiah via his school. She was deeply impressed by his academic accomplishments and the passion he possessed for his dream. He was interviewed, vetted, and impressed everyone on the board. He became a Seeds scholar, eventually graduating from college in four years.

Today, Isaiah works on Wall Street. He continues to dream how God may use his life for his glory. Only God knows where his dream may eventually lead.

Dominique lived on the east side of town. His neighborhood was a challenging place in which to live. With incessant regularity, peers tried to recruit him to join a gang. He steadfastly refused to do so. He knew that there was more for him in life.

Marilynn was introduced to Dominique by her jogging-buddy neighbor, Susan. She knew about the Seeds scholars program. She especially wanted Marilynn to know about Dominique's chess acumen. At that time, he was rated as one of the best chess players in the entire state.

Susan arranged for them to meet. Dominique's engaging personality and future dreams captivated Marilynn. She saw his potential in life. She took him to her committee, where he was interviewed, vetted, and chosen as a Seeds scholar. A godly mentor named Brian Henderson walked and worked closely with him.

Today, Dominique has graduated from college and is pursuing a vocation in physical therapy. His love for God has grown, and he's become an exceptional young man. He's inching closer and closer to becoming a grand master in chess as well.

Jasmine attended a Christian high school in Charlotte. She had a mom who sacrificed much for her success. And Jasmine had dreams of going to college. She had been on numerous mission trips. Her heart for the world was enormous.

The Seeds scholars program discovered Jasmine and interviewed her. She was awarded a scholarship, went to Clemson University, and has since graduated. She is still seeking exactly where God wants her vocationally. Most who know her are convinced she will one day be serving the Lord on the mission field.

And the list goes on and on. The Seeds scholar ministry continues with more and more success stories to this day. More than a dozen teens with dreams have been discovered and their gifts unleashed into the world. All because Marilynn and a few of her friends realized that $5000 a year and a mentor can change a teen's life.

They saw a need and filled it. They saw a hurt and healed it. They planted seeds of hope and watched them grow.

I hope I have honored Marilynn through the years by encouraging her to continue her fight for the underdog, the disenfranchised, the downtrodden, the needy, and the marginalized. I hope I have especially honored her by encouraging her to help teens with dreams.

Husband, think about the number of lives that could be changed through your wife's gifts being launched to serve others. Think about those changed lives rippling outward and touching many other lives as the years go by. They could number into the dozens—maybe hundreds. All because you took the time and made the effort to help encourage your wife to discover and launch her gifts to serve others.

If every husband everywhere did this, the world would be a much better and healthier place in which to live.

4

Respect Her Opinion

ANYONE WHO KNOWS ME will quickly acknowledge that sartorial splendor is not my forte. I'll never be on anyone's "best-dressed list." No one will ever seek me out to be on the cover of *GQ Magazine*.

Really, I'm not that bad. It's just that I've never been fashion-conscious—that has never been that important to me. I've never desired to impress others with my clothes. Why would I ever dress for success? After all, God looks at the heart! That was my position. But I did have some lessons to learn.

Forest Hill is a casual, come-as-you-are church. Therefore, I usually wear nice but casual slacks and a shirt—nothing particularly fashionable or noteworthy.

Once I was preparing for our Saturday night worship service. I dressed as usual. As I was making sure all was finally in order, Marilynn walked into the room. She paused for a moment as she scanned my attire. With a smile, she shook her head from side to side.

"Anything wrong?" I asked reluctantly.

She hesitated. Finally, I asked again. "C'mon, if something is not right, you need to be able to tell me what you are feeling."

"Okay," she responded with a hint of a giggle. "I don't think the way you are dressed looks right."

A bit defensively, I responded. "Don't you think what I'm wearing is okay? After all, we are a casual church. It's no big deal how I dress."

I continued this posture a bit longer, justifying why I was appropriately dressed.

Marilynn laughed and tried to wave it off, not wanting to exacerbate a confrontation. But inwardly I felt I needed to hear what she had to say. So I said something dangerous but necessary for all husbands to say to their wives. "Okay, I want to respect your opinion. I give you permission to say whatever you need to say. That's your right as my wife. Please tell me what you are thinking."

Finally, lightheartedly but also rightly balancing grace and truth, she responded, "David, this really isn't a big deal. But you asked my opinion. The way you are dressed kind of embarrasses me."

Her comment made me think twice. The way I dressed didn't just affect me. It affected her too. That's the essence of being one flesh. If she felt a bit embarrassed, I should feel embarrassed for her. I needed to hear her heart. I needed to respect her opinion.

Finally, I said to her, "Okay, you know clothes aren't that important to me. It's not what I know best. But what is important to me is that I respond empathetically to what you think. I need to understand what you are feeling. Tell me what's wrong. Help me to dress better."

"Okay," she said gladly. "I'd love to." She then pointed out things that should help me dress better. She went into my closet and helped me find better matches between pants and shirts. She encouraged certain belts, jackets, and sweaters during appropriate seasons. I actually enjoyed the tutorial!

After I finished dressing, I went to her for final approval before heading to the service. She smiled and gave me two thumbs up. Then I asked her if she would go shopping with me and help me pick out clothes that would never embarrass her again. She laughed and said yes.

We did so soon thereafter. It was actually a fun time for this guy who is fashion-challenged. I now have appropriately stocked my closet with clothes that go well together. Plus, I am now armed with much more knowledge from a wise wife about what does and doesn't match. One other positive thing came out of this encounter. The Saturday night service begins at 6:00. Usually, because we live close to the church, I don't need to leave until around 5:30 to get there on time. Marilynn and I now have an agreement that at promptly 5:15 I walk by her, my arms open wide, seeking a simple two thumbs up or two thumbs down. It is my pleasure to report to you that I now seldom receive two thumbs down.

All this happened because I wanted to respect Marilynn's opinion and not embarass her. I didn't ever want to embarrass Marilynn. I wanted to know her feelings.

I learned I honor her when I ask her opinion and she is able to tell me what she truly thinks. And often, I discover that her freely given and sought-after opinion not only greatly helps me be better, but it also deeply honors her.

We husbands are often "Captain Oblivious" with our wives. We live disconnected from them. They often have insights that could help us in many different areas. They are often transmitting signals to us. But, like radio waves needing a transmitter for sounds to be heard, we don't have our transmitters turned on. And if they are on, we have our dials set just a few numbers away from their signals. We only hear garbled gurgles and static sounds.

We husbands need to learn from our wives. We need to seek and respect their opinions. This respect comes more easily when we know them well.

GET TO KNOW YOUR WIFE WELL

Through the years, I've learned four different ways to know Marilynn well. They have helped me hear her transmissions. They have aided me in seeking her input. They have allowed me to clearly discern what she may be feeling and how I can digest what she may be trying to say to me. I know she has my best interests at heart. I know she wants my best. I know she desires my success. If so, and we are one flesh, wouldn't it be wise for me to learn better how to know her well?

These four ways are encapsulated in the acronym S-E-A-L. Think of them as ways to "seal the deal" with your wife—ways to know her well.

After all, the better you know her, the more you'll value her opinion.

And the closer you will become. She will feel honored. And when you finally seal the deal, the two of you truly become one—which is God's goal for all marriages.

Here it is:

S—Study her life

E—Empathize with her

A—Ask for her opinion

L—List what she says

Let's examine each one more closely.

Study Her Life

Someone once said that to be prepared is to succeed. That's true in most every area of life. And the key to being prepared is to study and learn.

Look at these words purportedly written by Solomon, the wisest man in the world:

> "Let the wise hear and increase in learning, and the one who understands obtain guidance" (Proverbs 1:5).

> "Whoever heeds instruction is on the path to life, but he who rejects reproof leads others astray" (Proverbs 10:17).

> "An intelligent heart acquires knowledge, and the ear of the wise seeks knowledge" (Proverbs 18:15).

The Bible clearly teaches that wise people need to study and learn.

Successful students know this truth. They know that the key to learning is taking the necessary time to study what they need to know. If they don't study the information, they will fail the tests. It's that simple.

Successful businesses know this truth. They put aside a percentage of their annual budgets for research and development. They carefully study what's been successful in the past in order to repeat it. They intricately study future trends in order to determine what will be successful. They know the importance of new innovations to remain on the cutting edge. They examine wasteful expenditures and eliminate them. They spend time and resources studying the competition. They ask if what they are doing is proving successful. Is there anything they need to emulate? Do better than others are doing? Successful businesses are in constant learning modes.

The same is true in athletics. Successful coaches carefully study the rules to look for any competitive advantage. They innovate and experiment so their teams will play better. They learn different techniques on how to motivate players. I know that my college basketball coach, Dean Smith, would spend countless hours studying our game films. He was always looking for ways to teach us how to become better players. He believed the maxim that "the eye in the sky doesn't lie." When players watch the video, there's no argument. Successful coaches and players are forever learning.

If the need for constant learning is essential for success in life, why not apply this same principle to our marriages? We husbands need to study our wives and learn about their unique giftedness and wisdom they have accrued through the years.

For example, we need to remember past situations where our wives gave us input that proved to be accurate. We need to appreciate their thought processes and how they reached their conclusions. Often their knowledge goes beyond mere women's intuition, a gift women uniquely possess. It's an earned wisdom accumulated through the years by study and experience.

We husbands should also ask friends about the strengths they see in our wives. I did this once with several members of my staff who work with Marilynn. They shared about difficult situations in which she had helped the team reach a consensus and the correct conclusion. I left that encounter with a new admiration for her. It made me appreciate more who she is and how she processes information and reaches conclusions. I had come to know her better.

We husbands also need to learn how we may have been too defensive toward or dismissive of our wives. If we have not taken our wives' opinions seriously in the past, we have thwarted their ability to speak truth into our lives in the present. We've stunted a grand opportunity to see blind spots be addressed and future growth to occur. We need to repent of our arrogance and reboot the learning process.

Wives aren't merely add-ons! They are gifts from God that help us grow and succeed. And if we are one flesh with them, when they speak to us based on their accumulated knowledge, they are speaking to us as a part of us. It's as if we were talking to ourselves with extremely wise words.

We'd be wise to study their lives.

Empathize with Her

To emphasize this point, I could quote the old Native American proverb, "Walk a mile in his moccasins." Or, as others say, "Jump inside that person's skin." Still another way to state the same truth is, "You just need to look at it from the other's perspective."

The word to describe this point is *empathy*. It's a concerted decision to walk in another's shoes, to jump inside another person's skin and try to understand life from her perspective. It's a biblical truth that is stated in many different places.

From the lips of Jesus: "Whatever you wish that others would do to you, do also to them, for this is the Law and the Prophets" (Matthew 7:12). That's empathy. Some call it the Golden Rule. It's golden because when empathy is practiced, relationships work.

From the pen of Paul: "Rejoice with those who rejoice, weep with those who weep" (Romans 12:15). This too is empathy. We feel what they feel. It's experiencing what they are experiencing from their point of view.

From the writings of Peter: "Finally, all of you, have unity of mind, sympathy, brotherly love, a tender heart, and a humble mind" (1 Peter 3:8). This adjuration comes right after husbands are told to honor their wives (verse 7). Do you see Peter's goal? It's unity. How does unity happen? It arrives through sympathy, love, a tender heart, and a humble mind. Unity (or oneness) comes through sympathy (and empathy), through trying to understand what another person is feeling. In the marriage relationship, empathy honors our wives.

If we husbands want to know our wives well, we need to develop empathy. How often do we do that? How often do we try to understand what it's like to chase little children around all day? And seldom have another adult with whom to converse? And often have a job on top of taking care of the kids? And have a monthly physiological cycle that changes the body's moods and perceptions? And perform all the other responsibilities that are expected of her?

If nothing else, the exercise of empathy helps a husband to develop a tender heart and a humble mind. It helps him develop a heart of compassion toward his wife and all women. It fights sexism and misogyny. It elevates all women in his eyes.

Above all, it honors his wife well.

Ask Her Opinion

My college basketball coach was a great teacher. What Coach Smith loved most about college basketball was not the actual game event, but teaching young men in practice how to play the game rightly.

After teaching us players something, he would invariably make a statement I've never forgotten. He'd ask us if we had any questions. Then he'd say, "Gentlemen, any question is a good question if you don't know the answer." He knew the only way we could ever learn was to ask questions—no matter how seemingly insignificant they may seem to us.

Surely Jesus felt the same way when he urged his followers, "Ask, and it will be given to you; seek, and you will find; knock, and it will be opened to you. For everyone who asks receives, and the one who seeks finds, and to the one who knocks it will be opened" (Matthew 7:7-8). He was saying the only way to have something is to first ask for it.

John was definitely echoing this same truth when he wrote, "This is the confidence that we have toward him, that if we ask anything according to his will he hears us" (1 John 5:14). Similarly, James states that we don't have because we don't ask (James 4:3).

To have, we need to ask. If we don't ask, we don't have. That's the clear teaching of the Bible.

It's true in our marriages too. In order to learn about our wives, we husbands need to ask them questions. For example, try to understand your wife's past and how it influences her present. Ask her opinion about issues of the day. Ask how she arrived at those conclusions. What books or blogs is she presently reading? Whom has she found particularly compelling? Who is influencing her thinking?

Then share with her some of the issues you are struggling with. It may be a difficult relationship. Or perhaps it's a problem at work. Or it may be an issue in local or world affairs. Ask her opinion. "What do you think I should do about this? How would you handle it? Do you have any insights that could help me?" She may not know the answer. She may not even be able to completely understand your problem. But she will deeply and sincerely appreciate the fact you asked. Indeed, she will feel honored that you respected her opinion enough to ask.

Especially, ask her what things you do that she likes. Then ask her what you do that she doesn't like. Get clarity if you need it. Find out the ways you embarrass and encourage her. Find out what she admires and doesn't admire. Ask for specifics. If you don't understand, ask again for more information and clarity.

The more you ask, the more you will learn about her and from her. Social psychologists incessantly tell us that a major way to make friends is to ask people questions about themselves. People love to talk about themselves. They love to know another person cares enough to ask. The willingness for one person to learn about another draws those two people closer together—and that's especially true in the marriage relationship.

Obviously, this means that when you ask your questions you are ready to listen. James 1:19 reads, "Know this, my beloved brothers: let every person be quick to hear, slow to speak, slow to anger." We do have two ears and only one mouth. Perhaps God was trying to suggest we should spend twice as much of our time listening rather than speaking?

And if we husbands are listening well, then we are ready for the next and final step necessary to seal the deal of knowing our wives well.

List What She Says

That's right—make a list. Write down what she says. Not only will this show you've truly listened, but more importantly, you'll be able to remember what she said. Doing this will help you to know your wife better. Be like Santa. Make your list. Check it twice. Find out how you've been naughty or nice with your wife.

Most people love lists. Marilynn does. She operates by them daily. It's a joke between us that if she doesn't have her list, she can't get anything done. There's even an app now on our smartphones that allows us to make lists. Written lists ensure we get things done and do them rightly.

God knew the importance of writing down information. To the prophet Habakkuk, he said, "Write the vision; make it plain on tablets, so he may run who reads it" (Habakkuk 2:2). God's message was to be a permanent witness, one to be fulfilled in the future, for people to be able to read for generations to come.

To Moses, God instructed, "Write these words, for in accordance with these words I have made a covenant with you and with Israel" (Exodus 34:27). This written word would be for all generations to read and know God's special, unique covenant with Israel.

Paul wrote, "Whatever was written in former days was written for our instruction, that through endurance and through the encouragement of the Scriptures we might have hope" (Romans 15:4). This includes all of the Old Testament Scriptures. God had prophets write down his words for the instruction and encouragement of his people in all places, for all times.

It could be argued that the Ten Commandments are God's ultimate written list!

If God knew the importance of writing down information and making lists, how much more should we husbands? Therefore, after having asked our wives for their opinions on different subjects, and having specifically heard what they have said, there is a next and final step. We husbands need "to seal the deal." How? By writing down a list of what we have heard.

I've tried to do this with Marilynn. Through the years, I've written down 20 things on my list that I've learned as I've listened to her. When followed, they make her feel honored. And they make us one.

1. I need her advice on the way I dress (she doesn't care how I dress around the house and in the places where I study—hooray!).

2. She feels honored when I ask her opinion about different subjects, issues, and concerns.

3. She loves looking forward to our day off together. It's like a weekly vacation time for her. Therefore, I need to make sure this day is sacred and guarded.

4. I need to let her tell me that she thinks I'm driving too fast or carelessly.

5. I don't need to take her corrections personally.

6. She loves it when I initiate prayer times together.

7. When she's telling me something that is painfully personal, she doesn't need me to offer a solution. She just wants me to listen and show I care.

8. She doesn't like to be left alone at a party. She feels awkward when having no one with whom to talk and is standing alone.

9. She wants me to take the initiative to leave a gathering or party. She doesn't like feeling like she's the one wanting us to leave.

10. If she fixes me dinner, then has to go out, it means a lot to her to see that the dishes are washed when she returns. That way, she feels I didn't take her for granted.

11. She loves it when I tell the kids, in her presence, how much I love, care for, and respect her.

12. She is deeply appreciative when I pay close attention to her gut instincts and intuition.

13. She doesn't ask for it, but she's surprised and pleased when I offer her the TV remote to choose the show she wants to watch.

14. It's really appreciated when I make the bed in the morning.

15. It's strictly forbidden to discuss marital problems with a person of the opposite sex. She is certain I honor this mutual commitment, as I am with her.

16. When I'm wrong, I should verbally say it—immediately. It means much less when I do so several days later.

17. I'm bigger and louder than she is. When I raise my voice, I may as well have a megaphone next to my mouth and her ear. She doesn't like it.

18. She loves to laugh with me over a cup of coffee when we remember fun times together. She especially loves it when we remember times with the kids (and now the grandkids!).

19. She loves it when I draw an imaginary circle on her arm, shoulder, or back when we are out in public. It's surreptitious. No one else can see it, or knows what it means. But the circle represents something that goes on and on. It's our way of saying to one another, even when we're in the presence of dozens, hundreds, or thousands, that we forever love one another. Our love for each other is like a circle. It will continue forever. Nothing will ever break it. It warms her heart when I do this.

20. She loves it when I scratch her back every night before we go to sleep. She may be asleep when I come to bed or vice versa, but I still scratch her back. When she's awake, I usually say, "I hope this back scratch is a small way of me erasing a way that I've previously hurt you." She always smiles when I say it. Then she encourages me to keep scratching her back.

I would imagine that several things on my list are also on yours. I'd also imagine that you'd have other items that I don't have. What's on the list isn't nearly as important as the fact that there is a list. Just make sure you have one.

We husbands need to S-E-A-L the deal. Study your wife. Empathize with her. Ask and respect her opinions. List what she says. Doing so will help you to know her well. It will prove you desire to honor her.

And the two become one flesh.

ONE MORE ILLUSTRATION

Early in our ministry together at Forest Hill, the church went through the Bethel Bible Study Series. It was designed to help people learn the Bible. A group of around twelve people would spend two years with me as the teacher of the curriculum. Then these twelve would each take a group of around twelve parishioners and teach them what I'd taught.

Marilynn was in that first group of twelve. She was a marvelous thinker and student. I enjoyed having her in the class.

At the end of the two years, I wanted to introduce the twelve to the congregation so they would know who their teachers would be. I stood up front in the sanctuary, going one by one down the row of the people in front of me who were facing the congregation. I got to Marilynn. Proudly, I informed all that she was my wife and a great student.

Then, without thinking (I do this often—speak before thinking), and stupidly trying to be humorous, I said, "And I want all of you to know that she's the only one of the twelve who slept with the teacher." There was a good laugh from those present. That only encouraged me to say more: "And I want all of you to know that she got nothing but A's in the class." There were a few more laughs.

Some didn't think what I said was funny. Later, one lady in the church told me she leaned over to her husband after my attempt at humor and said to him, "I now forgive you for anything and everything you've ever done to publicly embarrass me."

Upon arriving home after church, Marilynn was a bit distant. I asked her what was wrong. She simply said, "You kind of embarrassed me today." Callously, I asked, "What are you talking about?" She said, "Using me in your jokes."

"Captain Oblivious" became "Captain Obvious." Obviously, what I had done got a good laugh at her expense, but she felt hurt. Thankfully, she told me. Humbly and empathically, I listened. What I had done showed I didn't know her well in this area. I didn't honor her as I should have.

And in remembering this story, I probably should add #21 to my list: Don't ever publicly make your wife the brunt of a joke. It's not wise.

It will avoid much embarrassment—something I've obviously and wrongly done more than once in our marriage.

Mostly, it doesn't honor your wife.

And it keeps the two of you from becoming one.

Where Learning to Show Honor Begins

Do you know which one of the Ten Commandments is the first one to possess a promise?

Read these words from Ephesians 6:1-3: "Children, obey your parents in the Lord, for this is right. 'Honor your father and mother' (this is the first commandment with a promise), 'that it may go well with you and that you may live long in the land.'"

Paul urged all children to practice the positive duty of obeying their parents. It is the right thing to do because it conforms their lives to God's commandment. When they do obey it, they similarly honor their parents.

There's that pesky word *honor* again. Children are commanded by God to honor, prize, value, and esteem their parents.

God gives kids a reason to be motivated to choose to honor their parents. Again, this commandment was the first and only one of the Ten Commandments with a promise (Exodus 20:12). The promise is that if they would honor their parents, God would give them a long life in the land to where God was leading them. In Deuteronomy 5:16, God adds that if children honor their parents, it will go well for them in the land he's about to give them.

It's a general truth that Paul is giving here. Not every child who honors his parents is given long life, God's favor, and blessings. Not everything in life goes well for him. But generally, when children honor, prize, respect, esteem, and value their parents, they are giving evidence to a healthy home. Healthy homes generally produce healthy children. And healthy children generally live longer and give a nation a bright future and a hope.

Here is an important question to ponder: How do children learn to honor their parents? There are many different ways. But I'd suggest that the primary way is through the example of the way a husband honors his wife—especially in the kids' presence. I'd suggest that the way he honors his wife is key for how the children will honor them both.

That was certainly the case in my own home. Dad honored Mom. She was his valued treasure. He expected us kids to honor her as well. It was not conditional or optional. It was a mandate.

One special example stands out in my mind.

Overall, my dad was a gentle, kind, and sensitive man. He consistently showed God's love to us kids. But there was one moment in time when his gentleness turned to stern judgment. It happened in a moment when we kids started dishonoring Mom.

We were sitting around the lunch table after Sunday worship. One of our family traditions was our weekly lunch after the final service at the church. Mom would always fix an absolutely sumptuous feast. We would eat until we were full—and then some. She would always cap it off with a delicious dessert. After dessert, we'd spend a good hour or so just talking and laughing about anything and everything.

One Sunday, somehow, the conversation negatively and undeservedly turned toward Mom. She was a gracious, genteel, sensitive, Southern lady. She loved serving her family—as evidenced by the meals she regularly cooked for us. Her family was her life. That was undeniable.

But my brother, Howard, seized upon something that allowed him to start teasing her. I don't even remember what started it. But he began teasing her. My sister, Carolyn, and I jumped in as well. It soon escalated to disrespect and dishonor. Mom became quieter and quieter. Her embarrassment grew and grew.

Dad sensed Mom's discomfort. Their oneness caused him to feel what his beloved was feeling. He readily knew that our teasing had crossed the line to disrespect and dishonor. He didn't like it one bit. He had had enough. And he let us know it.

He turned to us kids, his voice raised a bit, and pointedly said, "That's enough! No more! I'll have you all know that you are dishonoring the woman I love. She is the most important person in my life. She means the world to me. Stop it right now. I mean it. I don't want to hear another word from any of you."

The teasing immediately stopped. We didn't say another word.

I vividly remember that moment to this day. It was a significant event in my life. My dad's response to us teasing Mom was an extremely important lesson for me to learn about my future as a husband and father.

Here's what I learned that day: Dad honored Mom by swiftly confronting our dishonoring her. And as I observed how he honored Mom in that moment, I was learning how to honor Marilynn in front of my kids. I was learning a way to produce healthy sons who would honor their wives and produce healthy children. I was helping our nation become stronger in the future.

Husband, it is very important for you to learn how to honor your wife in front of your kids—especially your sons. When you honor her in front of them, you are teaching them how to honor their future wives. You are helping to lay a solid foundation for their home's health and happiness. You are opening the door for God's favor and blessing in their families.

If you believe this is true, here are a few practical suggestions to help encourage your faithfulness in honoring your wives in front of your kids.

First, always speak well of your beloved in their presence. Let them hear from your lips how much you prize, esteem, respect, and admire your wife. Do this regularly. Let them hear from you how you'd marry her again in an instant. Let them listen to your stories of admiration about her and her gifts. Let them know she is one of your heroes in life.

When they roll their eyes upon hearing the same stories again and again, don't stop. Keep honoring your wife before them. Most teachers realize repetition is necessary in the classroom, and the same is true at home.

Second, don't ever speak down to your wife or severely reprimand her in their presence. Of course you will have times when you correct each other about certain things in a conversation in front of the children. That's normal and acceptable. The key is to never make your wife feel embarrassed or put her down in their presence. Don't make her feel like a second-class citizen in the family, or feel unimportant to you. Don't make her the brunt of insensitive jokes, making her look bad to the kids.

Third, if the kids ever come close to dishonoring her, rush to her aid. Make sure they know you are on her side. Never join them in dishonoring her. You are her defense and shield. You are her ally.

The kids feel the wrath of dad if mom is in the least way dishonored. This kind of "fear of dad" is a good thing. It motivates obedience. And they know what will happen if they dishonor mom. They have to deal with an angry dad who is defending his beloved. And they know that's never fun.

I've learned through the years that faith is much more caught than taught. For example, with my dad, I don't much remember the Bible verses he taught me. Or the sermons he preached. Or the prayers he prayed over me.

But I do remember seeing him seek God's Word for a solution to a personal or familial problem. I remember him regularly and persistently praying in times of need and plenty. I remember him visiting the sick and loving his congregants as they faced eternity, comforting them and giving them a heavenly hope in Jesus.

Though I don't remember much of what my dad said, I do remember how he lived. And it profoundly affected me. It motivated me to want what he had. I wanted to know the Lord he knew. I wanted to serve the Lord he served. Eventually, I caught his faith. And I'm a pastor like he was.

Similarly, kids will catch honor. God wants it to be highly contagious in the home. And this contagion begins with a husband faithfully honoring his wife. The sons will eventually catch it. They will choose to honor their wives. It will be passed on from generation to generation.

And, generally, your children and your children's children will live long in the land—experiencing God's presence and favor for years to come.

That alone is a huge reason and motivator for husbands to honor their wives.

5

Ask This Question Often

THE HEART OF THE matter is a matter of the heart. What wise words these are! Most all we do in life flows from what first happens in the heart.

Solomon echoes this truth with this poignant piece of wisdom: "Keep your heart with all vigilance, for from it flow the springs of life" (Proverbs 4:23). He knew the importance of the heart. He knew that everything in life flows from what's happening within. That's why a person needs to keep and guard the heart with all vigilance.

In our physical lives, a healthy heart usually means a healthy physical body. In the spiritual realm, it's similarly true. A healthy spiritual heart generally means a healthy spiritual life.

Jesus made the same point in Mark 7:20-23 when he said, "What comes out of a person is what defiles him. For from within, out of the heart of man, come evil thoughts, sexual immorality, theft, murder, adultery, coveting, wickedness, deceit, sensuality, envy, slander, pride, foolishness. All these evil things come from within, and they defile a person."

Everything in life, both good and evil, flows from the heart. The heart of the matter is a matter of the heart.

I'll never forget a counseling session I had with a couple. I asked for the husband and the wife to give their individual assessments of their marital problems. The wife didn't hesitate. She had her list. She ticked off each item, one by one.

After hearing the list, the husband began to take each item on the list and offer solutions. He knew the steps that needed to be taken for each problem to be fixed.

Exasperated, she finally looked at him and said, "You just don't get it, do you? I don't want you to fix the problems. I just want you! I want a relationship with you. I want to know you. I want to share life with you."

Finally, she bowed her head, tears in her eyes, and said, "I just want you to know what's going on in my heart."

Her last comment allows me to bring up another way we as husbands can honor our wives. It's not astrophysics. It's surprisingly simple, yet astonishingly significant to a woman. You need to ask your wife this question and ask it often: "How's your heart?" That's it. It's that simple. But, if asked sincerely and often, it can have profound and positive implications for a meaningful and successful marriage.

Remember: Your wife wants to be one with you. That was creation's design. That's what she desires most. But for oneness to occur, you must want it too. Your desire to honor and prize your wife will stimulate your desire to know her heart so that you can become one.

Husband, to do this is not natural. In your sinful, selfish condition, you are prone to abandon God's call to care for your wife's heart and place your desires above hers. You need to learn and practice being a servant. You need to value her life above your own. One specific way to do this is to ask her what's happening in her heart.

Before You Ask

But before you ask, here are two important things that need to happen first.

Desire Deep Friendship

The English language only has one word for *love*. It can be said by a lustful, hormone-charged teenager in the back seat of a car, or by a man in a hospital saying good-bye to his wife of more than 60 years, her mind wracked with the vicious disease called Alzheimer's. Having only one word to speak of such a broad range of feelings, emotions, or experiences can be very limiting. It doesn't allow us to communicate more specifically what we're talking about.

By contrast, ancient Greek had four different words for love. Each one referred to clearly different kinds of love.

One of those words is *philea*. This word refers to "friendship" love. The name of the city Philadelphia comes from the two Greek words: *philea* (friendship love) and *adelphos* (brothers). Philadelphia is, by its own name, "the city of brotherly love."

Remember that God wants a man and a woman to become one. That was his desire when he created marriage.

One of the best ways this can happen is by learning how to *philea* one another—that is, become each other's best friend. You enjoy each other. You desire to be with each other. You talk easily with one another. Though you have different interests, the time you spend together is precious and invaluable. If you have some time off, you can't wait to spend it with her. You treasure her. You prize her. You honor her by becoming her best friend.

Bottom line: It's easy to leave your spouse. It's impossible to leave your best friend.

Moreover, it's easy to ask your closest friend about the condition of her heart.

God knew the importance of husbands and wives bonding together as friends. Deuteronomy 24:5 reads, "When a man is newly married, he shall not go out with the army or be liable for any other public duty. He shall be free at home one year to be happy with his wife whom he has taken."

What a fascinating passage of Scripture! God knew the importance of a husband and wife building a strong relationship. Therefore, during that first, important, pliable, foundation-building year, God gave the husband freedom from all military service so he could focus on his wife and marriage. The commander of the army would never ask if this man was AWOL. He knew where he was. He was at home with his wife.

He was even free from all public duty. There was no jury duty. He didn't have to serve on community task forces. He was free from all committee work. He didn't have to volunteer for anything. During the first year of marriage, his job description was simple and concise: Be with your wife. Develop your relationship with her. Learn to honor her for the rest of your lives together.

In other words, learn and practice *philea* during this very important first year of marriage.

Before you ask your wife about the condition of her heart, first work on *philea*. Become her best friend. Enjoy your times with her. Cultivate the relationship.

A deep friendship allows conversations about the heart to happen more easily.

Pursue Her

Next, pursue your wife. During courtship, we men spend countless hours pursuing the woman we desire to marry. We put on our best front. We are creative with the time we spend together. We do everything we can to secure the "yes" from her. We pursue her with amazing intensity.

Then, soon after the marriage vows have been stated, the pursuit stops. The everyday routines of life take over. The predictable demands of daily living become habits of the heart. Before you know it, the kids have grown up and have left the home. You look across the dinner table and realize you're living with a stranger.

It shouldn't be this way! This was never God's intent for marriage. We men must learn to recapture the word *pursuit* in our marriages.

Hosea loved his wife Gomer. Even when she was a prostitute and left him, he continued to pursue her. Discovering her on a slave auction block, he outbid everyone else. He purchased and redeemed her. He brought her back home. In his actions, he said, "You need to know that I love you. If you leave me again, I'll pursue you again. If you leave me a thousand times, I'll pursue you a thousand times. My love for you is stronger than your wanderings."

The essence of love is pursuit. Again, we know what this means in the course of dating and courtship. And unfortunately, we soon lose it once married.

Making Time to Be Together

So how can we reclaim it? Here is the one thing that has worked for Marilynn and me through the years. It's not complicated. If you will do it, I promise it will rightly and properly guide you to the point you can ask your wife the most important question about her heart.

Have a weekly prolonged time together. That's it. Make sure you are never more than six days away from spending some in-depth, quality, meaningful time together.

A parenting guru once said something I've never forgotten. He said kids spell love T-I-M-E. He said if you want to give to and receive love from your kids, you must spend time with them. Before they ever receive presents, he said, they want your presence.

I've practiced that principle in my parenting. I've lived by the "five-years-from-now" rule. Five years from now, will someone remember if I was at a meeting, or a party, or a gathering? Probably not. But will my kids remember if I was at their sporting event, or dance recital, class presentation, or graduation? Probably so. Therefore, it's easy to see which event I should attend. My kids spell love T-I-M-E.

Therefore, I learned to write my kids' special events into my appointment calendar. Then when other people asked me if I was available during that time, I candidly responded, "Sorry, I have another appointment." I didn't explain the reason—that wasn't any of their business. They didn't need to know. But my kids knew. And that's what was most important to me.

If this principle is exceedingly important to practice with our kids (and it most assuredly is), shouldn't we also practice it with our wives? Don't wives also spell love T-I-M-E? How can we love our wives without spending time with them? Shouldn't that time alone with her be scheduled just like any other important appointment? Shouldn't this time together be guarded as more urgent than anything else vying for our attention?

That's why Marilynn and I schedule every Friday morning to be together. Nothing interferes with it. It's urgent for both of us. We look forward to it. She knows she is never more than six days away from being able to talk about something with me.

Why Friday? The church I pastor has a Saturday night service, and I spend all day Saturday preparing my message. On Sunday I must deliver the message two more times. I arrive home around one o'clock in the afternoon, and by then I'm absolutely exhausted. One study suggests that a 30-minute sermon, delivered passionately, is equal to running approximately 9 miles. If this study is accurate, that means that every weekend I run about 27 miles—about the same distance as a marathon! No wonder I'm exhausted every Sunday afternoon when I come home after church.

Because my weekends are furiously busy, filled with deadlines and responsibilities, Marilynn and I cannot be together during that time. At first we tried Mondays as our Sabbath day of rest. That didn't work because of all the things that piled up after a weekend. I ended up spending all day Monday thinking through all I had to do on Tuesdays once I arrived back in the office. Then we tried Tuesdays, but that made Wednesdays impossible.

So years ago we settled on Fridays. We actually get a bit of Saturday morning too, before I begin to focus on my sermon preparation for the evening service. It's a semblance of a weekend for us.

But we both look forward to Friday mornings. We go out together. We get a cup of coffee. We go find a quiet place where we can sip our coffee and talk. We'll go for a walk together. We pray together. I get caught up in her world. She asks about mine.

Taking Time to Share

It's then that I ask her the most important question I can ask as her husband: How is your heart? I really want to know. It's the wellspring of her life. I know that anything and everything that is happening to her dwells within her heart. As her closest friend, I want to know (this is what practicing *philea* looks like). She knows I'm pursuing her by asking this question. Whether the answer is good or bad, trivial or incidental, I want to know how her heart is.

Sometimes she simply says, "I'm doing fine." And we go on to talk about other things. Other times she openly shares some deep places of anguish and pain. She knows she has permission to share with me whatever she needs to say. I am there for her. I care for her. I want to hear her heart. I want to know what's rummaging inside her head.

I probably should add this caveat at this point: There are some times when, after a long, hard week's work, I can't give Marilynn what she needs. Although it doesn't happen often, it does happen. When it does, I have to be honest with her. I say, "I hope you understand. This week has been extremely hard. I just don't have anything to give you. My tank is empty. There is no reserve. I'm sorry."

When this happens, she responds with grace. Most often, if she still needs to share something with me, she knows it can be done in a day or two. We have an agreement between us that when I'm absolutely exhausted, Marilynn gives me grace and space. I don't want to misuse our time alone. I want to know her heart. But occasionally there are times when I simply have nothing to give. And Marilynn understands.

A couple of times Marilynn has not read me well. She would begin to share a burden before realizing I couldn't shoulder another problem. It has caused tension. I don't respond well. Over the years, we've learned to read each other's caution lights blinking when one or the other of us is extremely fatigued.

However, most of the time, I'm able and ready to listen to Marilynn's heart. I've provided the safe environment in which she can say anything. She is free to express herself as the unique and beautiful creature she is.

And I'm ready to hear her heart.

Ask the Question—Then Listen

It is in this safe environment, during the set-aside weekly time together, that you can ask your wife this essential and important question: How is your heart?

Once you've said that, then it's your job to listen. First Peter 3:7 says that we husbands should live with our wives "in an understanding way." That means we spend time and effort truly trying to understand what is taking place in her. It means listening intently.

The book of Job tells the story of a man who underwent extraordinary suffering. He lost his family, finances, and health in one fell swoop. What he went through is unimaginable to the modern-day reader.

Some friends came to visit him. At first, they sat silently with him. Good for them! Then they started pontificating on the reasons that Job was suffering. Mostly, they suggested that there was unconfessed sin in his heart. Therefore, God must be punishing him. After hearing their diatribes, Job suggested he liked it much better when they just sat silently with him.

Jan Harrison went through a Job-like experience. Her son James was in Africa, serving the needy and caring for the hurting. He contracted a severe case of pneumonia. It cost him his life. The grief she and her husband Frank went through was unbearable. She wrote a book describing her journey, entitled *Life After the Storm: God Will Carry You Through*. It's an amazingly powerful book of God's redemption in tragedy.

I had Jan on my local radio show on WBT in Charlotte, North Carolina. She described her grief in vivid detail. She shared about the people who came by her house and cared for her and Frank. I asked her, "What things did people say that helped you the most?"

She paused before answering. Finally, she said, "Nothing." I raised my eyebrows. She could tell I didn't understand. She smiled, then continued. "David, the people who cared for us the best were the people who said nothing. They were simply there. They touched us physically to express compassion. Then they listened. They listened intently to the pain and grief in our hearts. They didn't try to solve the situation. They couldn't. They didn't try to explain it biblically or theologically.

They couldn't. Those who meant the most to us in our grief were those who simply came and listened to our pain and hurt."

After you ask your wife how her heart is doing, listen. Just hear what she says. Don't analyze her. Don't try to fix her. Don't try to give insights to her. Just listen to the words flowing from her heart.

When you do need to say something, wait until after you have identified her feelings. Listen especially and intently for her "feeling" words. I learned about this approach when I was a graduate counseling student at the University of Florida. Most every good therapist does this. It's an easy way to get someone to open up.

But the approach isn't limited to a counselor. Anyone can do it. Anyone can practice it. Everyone should do it!

Simply listen intently for your wife's feeling words. They are easy to spot. They are words like *sad, angry, frustrated, hurt, disappointed, unworthy, discouraged, purposeless, overwhelmed, empty, useless,* etc.

Or, on the positive side, they may be words like *happy, joyful, glad, excited, encouraged, edified, redeemed, rewarded, passionate, stoked, energized, hopeful,* etc.

Believe me, those feeling words are there. They are present. They are in every sentence we speak. They are foundational for understanding the heart. They are in your own heart at different times in your life. In fact, a meaningful exercise may be for you to list out feeling words you know are in your heart. This will help you better listen for those words as they are spoken from your wife's heart.

To aid in your listening to her heart, here are a few more tips:

1. Look her in the eye. Eyes often communicate as much, if not more, than words. Remain riveted on her eyes. This will help her to open her heart.

2. Hold her hand. Human touch is a special way of communicating. It says you care for her heart.

3. Make sure any touching is nonsexual. You are not listening as a quid pro quo for sexual favors later on. If so, you are abusing the intimacy of the moment.

Then, when it's time for you to speak, reflect on those feeling words. Say them back to her. Say something like, "It sounds like you're feeling pretty empty right now." Or whatever the feeling word is.

If you miss the right feeling word, don't worry. Your wife will correct you. She will let you know you missed it. "No, I think I'm feeling more like _____." When she tells you the correct feeling word, then you can rightly reflect it.

When you do nail the right word, watch her face light up! Most often, you'll see a smile and hear an excited "Yes, that's it!" from her. Then she may go a bit deeper with her feelings. If so, listen more intently. Or she may be satisfied that she's been heard. She will let you know, especially when she feels you have heard her heart.

A FEW QUALIFIERS

I need to add a few qualifiers here. Hopefully, they will help defuse the three major questions asked of me when I teach this.

First, am I not becoming a woman by doing this? I'm asked, "Is this the gobbledygook I read about men getting in touch with their feminine emotions?"

Of course not! It's a man getting in touch with his wife's emotions. It's learning how to serve, not be served. Marriage is the PhD program for learning to be a servant. It's graduate-level training. You are learning how to empathize with the person you love the most in the world even in the areas in which you are radically different from her. However, if in the process you learn how to get in touch with your own emotions, so much the better!

The second question is, "What if my wife is emotionally damaged from her past? What if I'm inadequately equipped to handle her emotional state? I can't be her therapist. Simply listening to her feeling words is not going to help her. She needs far more than I can give."

If this is the case, you may need to guide your wife to a professional counselor. You may need to help her get the help she needs. You are correct: You can't be her therapist if she is severely damaged from her past. She may even see you as part of her problem—if not the entire problem.

When you realize your capabilities as a listening and caring husband are inadequate, you must get her the help she needs and not feel guilty—and be personally present with the counselor, if necessary.

In giving this advice on listening, I'm assuming you are in a relatively healthy relationship. You are both functional. You are both living life together as well as possible in a very broken world. When this is the case, listening for feeling words to hear your wife's heart is very beneficial.

Third, I'm asked, "What if she doesn't respond to my pursuit of her? What if she distances herself from me? What if she won't open up her heart to me? Then what can I do?"

I have a friend who is in this very position. His wife of 30 years just left him. He doesn't know all that he did wrong. He is willing to own up to what he did, but she won't tell him. He has pursued her on many different occasions. But she constantly rebuffs his overtures toward her. He would love to talk to her. He would love to hear her feelings. He hungers for reconciliation and desires it for his kids. But mostly he wants it for the glory of God.

The only answer can be to pursue her in prayer. Ask God to open her heart. Continue to become the man and husband God wants you to become. Be Hosea in your prayers. Pursue the wife of your youth in your talks with God. Then pray some more. Pray without ceasing (1 Thessalonians 5:17). Remember that one day you must appear before God and answer for your life. You're not responsible for hers, only yours. Therefore, you must be faithful as much as is possible.

And if the situation ever arises, and God, in his eternal grace, mercy, and goodness opens the door again for you to be one with her, then make sure you take her hand, look her in the eye, and ask the most important question any husband can ask his wife: "How's your heart?"

Then reassure her you really want to know. It will draw you closer to one another than anything else you could do.

REMEMBER TO ASK OFTEN

Your wife really does want to speak to you from her heart. She wants to know that you care about her. She wants to feel honored by a listening ear—something she desires especially from you. She knows it will draw her closer to you. She knows it will help make you one—God's intent when he created marriage.

She wants you to ask this question often: "How's your heart?"

That's because the heart of the matter is a matter of the heart.

Honor Through De-Escalation

The Old Testament teaches "eye for eye, tooth for tooth" (Exodus 21:24). It's called *lex talionis,* or "the law of retaliation." It means tit for tat. Whatever you do to me, I, in turn, can do the same to you.

It was a way of maintaining justice and purging evil. It is still practiced in some cultures today. It's supposedly a deterrent to crime—especially when the criminal knows the stiff penalty he faces if caught for his crime.

Interestingly, some would argue that *lex talionis* is filled with grace. That's because most retaliation never stops at merely giving back what was taken in kind. Most retaliation is angrily motivated to escalate the offense. It strikes back harder than the way someone was struck. It steals more than was stolen. It kills more than was killed. It hurts more than was hurt. It's filled with revenge.

The source of most genocide and tribalism is an escalating *lex talionis.* A person is killed. Anger rises among members of the tribe that lost one of its members. Revenge is demanded. So the tribe retaliates and kills two members of the other tribe. More revenge is enacted and several members of the other tribe are killed. The cycle of revenge killing escalates. Eventually, dozens, hundreds, even thousands of lives are lost. Genocide, the attempted elimination of an entire tribe, sadly becomes the eventual outcome.

That's why some would argue that God's intention for *lex talionis* is filled with grace. Its original design was to prevent the increasing escalation of revenge killing. By grace, God wanted justice to allow only one eye for another person's eye, and only one tooth for another person's tooth.

Realistically, however, that seldom happens. Human nature doesn't work that way. It seldom wants an exact revenge. It wants the person who hurt me to suffer more than I did. It wants the other person to experience more pain than I experienced.

That's why the best way to thwart the increasing escalation of revenge killing is to practice what Jesus said in Matthew 5:38-39: "You have heard that it was said, 'An eye for an eye and a tooth for a tooth.' But I say to you, Do not resist the one who is evil. But if anyone slaps you on the right cheek, turn to him the other also."

Jesus was confronting individual conduct amidst the universal urge for an escalating, personal revenge. Since most people are right-handed, the backhanded slap was the ultimate insult. Thus Jesus was addressing the necessity to thwart escalating violence—one that motivates a more potent counterattack on the person who deeply offended me.

What does this have to do with a husband honoring his wife? Plenty. It speaks to the need for husbands to learn how to practice honor by de-escalating conflict when it arises in marriage. It speaks to husbands about practicing what that inestimable theologian, Barney Fife, constantly counseled on *The Andy Griffith Show:* "Nip it in the bud."

In other words, Deputy Fife was trying to teach us the need to stop the problem before it starts. Jesus was trying to teach us this same truth when he taught us to turn the other cheek. He gave the same principle in another verse: "If your right eye causes you to sin, tear it out and throw it away" (Matthew 5:29).

Interestingly, this principle was given in the context of stopping lust that may lead to adultery. The eye is the pathway by which most temptation occurs in a husband's life. This verse has nothing to do with bodily mutilation. Rather, Jesus gave a purposeful hyperbole that communicated a specific way that a man is to honor his wife. Everything that potentially can lead him to infidelity should be nipped in the bud.

To honor his wife, a husband needs to stop all temptations before they start.

In marriage, angry arguments rarely begin with heightened, intense anger. Usually they start when one or both individuals are tired and ultrasensitive. Defenses are broken down and emotions are easily irritated. The husband and wife are vulnerable.

The argument commences with a small offense. The offended spouse's response to the offense is exaggerated. Then the other responds with a bit more ferocity. Before you know it, verbal grenades are being launched back and forth, destructively exploding with each new word.

Both husband and wife say words they never mean to say. But they are said. They wound deeply. And they are regrettably lodged in each other's memory banks for weeks, sometimes even for years to come, specifically remembered when the next offense occurs.

Husband, there are ways you can stop these arguments before they start and keep the offenses from escalating. You can nip them in the bud and prevent verbal destruction and pain. You can honor your wife simply by practicing a couple of disciplines.

What are they? Both disciplines are from friends who have learned the value of de-escalation in honoring their wives.

First, one husband de-escalates potential fights with his wife by agreeing to speak key words that signal when escalation is happening. The words always have to do with water. That's because both of them love lakes, streams, and oceans.

Whenever either of them uses a "water" word as an argument grows, the other must immediately stop the escalation. They must push the pause button on the argument. Neither can say anything else. This "calming down" time allows both of them to stop the escalation, assess the situation, and try to nip it in the bud.

The husband tells me this tip toward de-escalation has prevented many an angry word and a scorched-earth argument between them. He adds that when he does this, his wife feels honored and appreciated by their previously agreed-to mutual decision.

They now find themselves actually laughing in the middle of a potentially tense argument when the water word is spoken.

Determine your own key words, and try this and see if it doesn't work for you as well.

Another husband told me how he practices de-escalation in his marriage. He has written down a list of all the things his wife has done for him and all that he appreciates about her. It's specific, detailed, and several pages long. It was written during a time when he was feeling deep affection and appreciation for her. He keeps the list in a desk drawer in his home.

When arguments escalate with his wife, he has an inner alarm bell that sounds. He knows they are headed toward a destructive conflict. That's when he literally gives his wife the "time-out" sign that coaches give officials in sporting contests. She nods in agreement. She knows what he is going to do next.

He goes into another room, opens his desk drawer, and pulls out his list. For the next several minutes, he repeatedly reads all he likes and appreciates about his wife. Over and over again, he lets his own written words counsel his soul. Sometimes he even reads his words out loud to himself.

The more he reads, the more his heart is soothed and warmed. He calms down. He returns to the room and expresses love and appreciation to her. He thanks her for all she has meant to him. He apologizes. The argument is nipped in the bud. They embrace and she feels honored. They move more toward oneness.

I'm certain there are other ways to de-escalate conflict. These two have worked for my friends and they swear by them. If you can take a few moments to think of others, please do. Just make sure you practice them. Do whatever you need to do to stop the escalation.

That's because *lex talionis* simply doesn't work. The human heart's preponderance toward pride and its desire for revenge won't allow a sole tit for tat. There's always escalation.

Lex talionis doesn't work with personal hurts. Nor does it work with tribalism. And it doesn't work in marriage.

The only answer can be de-escalation. When properly practiced by a husband, it will lead to his wife feeling honored. When this happens, forgiveness flows. When forgiveness is flowing, God's great grace abounds.

And a husband/wife relationship where grace is in place always produces the healthiest possible marriage—a marriage where the husband honors his wife and the two live out their oneness.

6

Share Your Heart

It was the most difficult time I'd ever experienced in ministry. About ten years into my leadership at Forest Hill, I attempted to take the church through a time of transition. I initially thought that I'd communicated well what I wanted to do. I had spent an entire weekend with the leaders of the church, and I thought I had unanimous buy-in.

Initial implementation seemed to go well. There were a few questions from different people. But that didn't surprise or concern me. That should be expected when change is about to take place.

But as weeks poured into a few months, questions became protests. People who were once my supporters became my critics. And the number of critics seemed to grow every day. Over time, I felt increasingly alone and discouraged. I wasn't exactly sure what I needed to do next.

Sensing my frustration and need for rest, one of Forest Hill's members arranged for Marilynn and me to escape for a week at the beach. I knew I needed the break. I was hoping that this week away would allow me to clear my mind and regain energy.

I had failed to realize just how much the stress over the past several months had deteriorated my stamina. On the first night away, I couldn't sleep. After a couple of hours of fitful attempts at sleep, I sat up in bed and let out a deep sigh. I looked out over the water, feeling emotionally paralyzed, contemplating the situation and wondering whether I could ever move forward again.

Marilynn awakened at the sound of my sigh. With enormous sensitivity, she asked, "You're not doing well, are you?"

"No, I'm not," I responded.

There were several moments of silence that ensued. She was uncertain what to say next, as was I. She reached her hand over to mine and squeezed it. Finally, she said, "Please tell me what's going on."

I didn't want to. Men and husbands aren't supposed to share their hearts. I was raised to believe that big boys don't cry. Men are supposed to be strong. They are to lead their families with force. They are supposed to never give up. Their wives are supposed to admire their dogged, relentless strength and perseverance.

"Please tell me what you are feeling," Marilynn persisted.

The dam burst. Tears flowed. Like a blister being burst, all the pent-up pus of months of frustration and fatigue oozed forth. The more I talked, the more my feelings poured forth. When I finished, I breathed another deep sigh.

Then I began to feel embarrassment. Marilynn had seen me at my weakest moment. I had shared a depth of feeling I'd never shared before. I was certain she thought less of me. I knew she was now officially embarrassed to be my wife. She shocked me with her response.

"David, I believe in you." Then she squeezed my hand again and said it again. "I believe in you."

That's all she said. That's all she needed to say. Renewed confidence pulsated within. Hope surged in my soul. I began to believe this problem was solvable. I knew my leadership was damaged but not destroyed.

Since this incident that happened more than twenty years ago, Forest Hill has become a very strong church. Its witness is felt around the world. I'm honored to be its pastor. But its success can be directly attributed to my wife speaking five words to me on a much-needed vacation: "David, I believe in you."

But before Marilynn could speak these words to me, I had to learn a very valuable lesson. I had to squash the lie that men never cry. I had to kill my prideful attitude that believed I always needed to be strong.

I had to buy the truth that Marilynn really wanted to hear what was on my heart. She desired to be strong when I was weak. She felt called to help me carry my burdens. But it couldn't happen unless I was willing to share my heart with her.

YOUR WIFE IS YOUR *EZER*

In Genesis 2:18, God said it's not good for man to be alone. Therefore, he created Eve for Adam. She was called his helper. The word in the original Hebrew text is *ezer.* I'm not sure helper gives the full understanding of what this word means.

In other places in the Bible, the word *ezer* describes God himself. When done, it describes God as a helper, rock, or our strength. For example, God is the *ezer* of the fatherless (Psalm 10:14). He was King David's *ezer* and deliverer (Psalm 70:5). In Deuteronomy 33:29, God was described in military terms as one's shield and *ezer* and a glorious sword. In fact, on three different occasions in the Bible the word *ezer* is used to describe God in a military context.

In my opinion, thinking of Eve as a rock, or strength, or a military fighter, or a protector gives all wives an added importance in the marriage relationship. Wives are not mere companions. They are not simply passive bystanders. Their responsibility isn't limited to just supporting their husbands in life's endeavors.

To the contrary! They are rocks on whom a husband can lean when he is experiencing life's difficult trials. They are sources of strength when a husband feels too listless to fight. They will fight for him, as Marilynn did for me on that fateful evening at the beach, giving help, strength, and courage.

In Genesis 2:18, the word *ezer* is combined with the Hebrew word *kenegdo* to give even more specificity as to why Eve was created. *Kenegdo* implies being equal to and one with. It implies that she came from the man's side only to become one with him again in marriage.

Therefore, when you place these two words together, it's easy to see how wrongly and inadequately the term "helpmate" is to describe the woman. Literally it implies a rock and strength of the same nature. It implies equality, mutuality, and harmony with the husband.

In other words, the wife was created by God to be her husband's rock, strength, and helper. When she fulfills this role, she brings equality, mutuality, harmony, and...oneness. When the wife is operating as an *ezer/kenegdo*, she is allowing God's desire for all marriages to occur: two become one.

Yes, she's sensitive. Many husbands have failed to realize just how sensitive their wives are. Sometimes they wrongly equate this sensitivity to weakness.

But I'm convinced this sensitivity is a part of God's beautiful *ezer* in the wife. Her sensitivity is her strength. It's what moves her to stay up with sick kids all night and fight for their health. She does the same thing for you too! It's what makes her defend you when others are critical. It's what compels her to stand by you no matter what.

That's why you need to share your heart with your wife. When you don't, it makes her think there's something wrong between you. That's part of her sensitivity too. She feels fear, wondering if there's a fissure in your *kenegdo,* your oneness. If you sense she thinks something is wrong between you, let her know nothing is wrong. Then, when you are able to open up and share what is happening in your heart, she will be your *ezer*, your rock.

Husband, you show love to your wife by sharing your heart. Ephesians 5:33 states that a husband is to love his wife. It's apparently her greatest need in the relationship. When a husband really loves his wife, he shares his heart with her. He knows she is a source of stealth strength. He knows she wants to fight for him and what he's going through. He knows she feels honored to do so. When all this happens, you two will move closer to one another.

You will become one as she operates as *ezer/kenegdo*.

If Only

They had everything. They were both attractive and had dynamic careers. They had beautiful children. On the outside, it was a picturesque marriage. But they were now separated, seriously contemplating divorce.

What had happened? Over the years, as lovers and married partners, they had failed to follow the clear adjuration of Song of Solomon 2:15. They had failed to catch the little foxes that were ruining their marriage vineyard. The husband especially had allowed bitterness after bitterness to accumulate in his heart.

By the time they entered my office for marriage counseling, they were regularly sniping at each other. Every misinterpreted gesture, every raised voice only antagonized the other. She was much better than he at verbal assaults. After a few failed attempts at volleying a verbal grenade back at her, he went into his cave.

Her voice became louder and louder. He retreated deeper into his silence. She tried every verbal trick, to no avail.

They both looked to me for an answer. Finally, I said to him, "You are really hurting right now, aren't you?" He nodded. I continued, "Your pain right now is not just because of the last few minutes of her expressed anger, is it? It's built up over some time, hasn't it?" He nodded.

Then I asked if he'd be willing to take her out for coffee sometime during the next week. I urged him to share his heart with her. I wanted him to tell her everything that he was feeling. I asked her if she would be willing to listen—even if she was the source of some or much of his pain. She hesitated for a moment. Then she turned to him and asked, "Would you be willing to do this?"

He also paused. Finally, he said he would. "You really would?" she asked again. He assured her he would. "Yes, I'd love to hear your heart. You can say anything. Just let me know what you are going through. I want to be there for you. I want to fight for you. I want to help you."

They left my office talking. She was vibrant, buoyed with hope.

A week later, only she returned. She sadly said he wasn't coming. She looked downtrodden, bedraggled, forlorn, defeated.

I asked how the coffee time went. She said he never called. She sighed, feeling the weight of what now seemed like an inevitable divorce.

Then she said something startling to me. "You know, David, I'd have been willing to hear him say anything he wanted to say to me. I would have listened. I was ready to own up to my part of the problem—perhaps even taking more blame than I should have. I just wanted him to start talking to me. I just wanted him to open up to me. I wanted him to share his heart with me. I wanted to help him in any way I could. If only he had shared his heart."

She had wanted the mysterious beauty of oneness. She had wanted their lives to be blessedly intermixed together.

THE ROAD TO ONENESS

God's design, from the moment man and woman were created, was that they would leave their parents, make public vows of permanent commitment to one another, and seal this covenant with a sexual union. The result of this is oneness. Two people "become one flesh" (Genesis 2:24). This is a creation mandate. It's God's will for all marriages.

When Jesus was confronted with a prickly debate about divorce, his response was that divorce (the opposite of oneness) was never God's original intent in creation. It's the result of humanity's brokenness and selfishness. "Have you not read that he who created them from the beginning made them male and female...?" he asked. Then he quoted Genesis 2:24 (Matthew 19:4-5). Immediately thereafter, Jesus remarkably proclaimed, "So they are no longer two but one flesh. What therefore God has joined together, let not man separate" (verse 6).

Jesus was very clear. The goal of marriage is oneness. What God has inextricably joined together as one, no person should ever attempt to separate. No flesh-and-blood person should tear apart two hearts joined together by God.

I'm convinced that this oneness between a husband and a wife can't occur unless the husband is willing to share his heart. He must be willing to be vulnerable. He must fight the lie that sharing feelings exposes weakness.

When a husband is willing to be vulnerable and share his heart, his wife has the opportunity to shift into her *ezer* role. He will see her become his rock, helper, support, strength, and warrior to help him move forward in his life.

In all this, his heart will become more one with hers. Her heart will become more one with his. His load will be lightened. She will feel needed and honored in the relationship. They will share harmony and mutuality—*kenegdo*. Nothing in life will be so big that they can't face it together.

WAYS TO CONNECT

If your wife yearns to know what's happening in your heart, it won't happen by fiat. Don't hope it will somehow happen without you being intentional about it. You need to think through specific times when you can talk. You need to look for opportunities when sharing your heart will be comfortable and natural.

Here are some practical suggestions that have proven successful. Remember that your wife desires to be one with you. She wants to connect with you. That's her heart's desire. She really yearns for it to happen.

Therefore, when you arrive home from work, instead of flopping on the couch and mindlessly watching the television, take a few moments to intentionally sit and talk with her. Perhaps it's as one or both of you prepare dinner. Ask her about her heart and what she's feeling. When she senses your sincere desire to connect with her, that will naturally open up an opportunity for you to share your heart with her.

Another practical suggestion is that you set up a weekly date time. As I stated earlier, Marilynn and I consider this essential for a successful marriage. We constantly adjure couples to make sure they have a weekly time together—a time when it's just the two of you alone. You focus solely on one another. She knows she is a priority for you. She knows you greatly admire her intellect and insights—especially into your life. You recognize that she knows you well and you need her thoughts.

Whatever you do, make sure this time isn't spent entertaining yourselves in such a way that you aren't able to talk to one another. Movies and television are great for idle enjoyment, but they don't allow for you to have any conversations. Make sure you are face-to-face, and that you can talk and share. Go out for dinner together. Looking into her eyes over a meal fosters more intimacy. The way you smile at her will often say more than words could ever express. Hold her hand. Squeeze it when making a point. Make sure you ask about her heart. Then be ready, willing, and able to share yours with her.

Be intentional throughout the week about making opportunities to be together. This could mean a car ride, going to an evening gathering together, or both of you going out for a walk immediately after you arrive home from work. You could even try to have a quick conversation before you go to sleep at night. Or, after an intimate time of making love together, you could have "pillow talk," a time during which you are both vulnerable and willing to share your heart.

Just make sure to always ask about her heart. Then be ready and willing to share your own. For both of you to do this will draw you closer together. Every wife hopes her husband will practice Song of Solomon 2:10: "My beloved speaks...to me." It should begin in courtship. It's supposed to continue in greater depth all through your marriage. When you do this, the two of you will become one.

The Feeling Words

Before you share your heart, here is another very practical but helpful exercise. Get in touch with your own heart. Listen to what's happening inside you. Take out a piece of paper and pen and start listing your feelings. Yes, put them down on paper. The more you can identify, the better off you'll be.

Be still and know that God is inside you. He wants you to get in touch with your inner man. He created you. He knows even better than you do what you are feeling. Jesus said his sheep hear his voice (John 10:27). Listen to his still, small voice within you.

Write your emotions down on the paper, "I feel _____ _____."

Angry...depressed...frustrated...demoralized...helpless...like a failure...ready to give up...overwhelmed...discouraged...weak...insignificant...hopeless...

What is it you really feel? Only you and the Lord know. Your feelings will be revealed to you if you truly desire to know them. But make sure you know them. It's imperative you do. Writing them down helps you know them. You obviously can't share your heart if you don't know your heart!

One exercise that some men have found helpful is to write their wife a letter expressing as many of their discovered feeling words as possible. One man wrote this letter:

> Hi honey! I hope you are well. I really do love you—even though I don't express feelings very well. You know this. Anyway, I just wanted to let you know that this week I've been really tired, even exhausted. I'm overwhelmed at work. I'm wondering if I'm underperforming and my boss is really upset with me. Then I move a bit toward feeling depressed. I don't want to share these feelings with you because I think you'll think less of me. But I've been told you actually want to help me, be strong for me, even fight for me. So I'm writing this letter to let you know my heart and seeking your help because I really do believe you want to be my helper. I feel deep love for you. Please know it's true.

He then sent the letter to her. Notice his intentionality in listing his feeling words: love, tired, exhausted, overwhelmed, wondering, underperforming, and depressed. When they finally had some alone time together, you can imagine how the floodgates opened. The letter primed his emotional pump. That's what helped him to share his heart. Any fear he might have had up to this point was vanquished by the letter. Everything thereafter flowed naturally between them.

A Wonderful Benefit

Husbands should not share their hearts with their wives for the side benefit I'm about to mention. But it is nevertheless a wonderful benefit. When you share your heart openly and honestly with your wife, it draws her closer to you. It increases intimacy. The closer she feels to you, the more she will be drawn to you sexually. But don't share your heart to receive sex from your wife. This isn't a quid pro quo. Your wife isn't a dummy. If you attempt to do this, she will see readily through the façade.

But when she sees authentic emotions pouring from your heart, she will be drawn to you. Her sensitive, empathetic nature will move toward you. It's only natural that in response to you loving her by sharing your heart, she would then want to express herself physically to you. That's one way she says, "I love you too."

And this increases oneness as well.

A Natural Question

Here's a question that frequently arises whenever I encourage husbands to share their hearts with their wives. "David," I'm asked, "what if she is the source of the emotions I am feeling? For me to say anything to her will only cause a confrontation."

My answer is twofold. First, if the feelings are deep and unresolved and they've been building up over years, you probably need to get professional help. You may need to find a counselor with whom you can both process your feelings (I bet she has some emotions toward you too if you've reached this point in your marriage).

Second, if the feelings are not deep and unresolved but merely the result of two selfish people living together, find a time when both of you can safely share your hearts. It's most likely a time when you are both feeling rested, and when you are both ready and willing to move toward one another in complete honesty. Mostly, you desire to be one.

Conflict in a marriage is not necessarily bad. My dad repeatedly said that conflict is the pathway to intimacy. He said it should never be feared. Conflict shows there's a rock in the middle of your marriage road. It's an opportunity for you to work together at removing the rock so the marital ride can advance more smoothly. When you remove it together, you'll be drawn closer together.

Just make sure you avoid the poison of the "root of bitterness" (Hebrews 12:15). Bitterness occurs when a hurt feeling is allowed to persist and fester deep within. If left alone, it can defile and eventually destroy a marriage. Make sure you remove the root of bitterness before it becomes a kudzu of conflict.

And the only way that can happen is by being willing to share your heart.

Your Most Valuable Trophy

After completing my four years of playing varsity basketball at the University of North Carolina, I received an incredible opportunity to continue my playing career in the European basketball leagues. More specifically, I signed a contract and played for two years with a professional basketball team located in Nice, France, on the French Riviera.

Okay, I already hear the guffaws and laughter. I know what you're thinking. You're saying I probably needed to go into the ministry after two years as a single guy playing professional basketball on the French Riviera!

Well, it was fun. I did have a good time. But these were also life-changing years for me. I was all alone and on my own. I had to grow up quickly in a place I knew little about.

I was dropped in the middle of the French culture with a modicum of understanding of the language. I had taken high school French, but I didn't know the language well. And my new French friends and teammates steadfastly refused to speak English with me, even though several spoke English well. From day one, they told me I had to learn their language and culture. It was total immersion.

Within months, I was fairly fluent in French. That doesn't mean there weren't moments of total embarrassment before fluency occurred.

For example, one night I was invited to the team president's house for dinner with several other teammates and their spouses. It was a sumptuous seven-course meal. The French generally don't eat quickly. They savor every morsel, every bite of food. And they did so that evening. The meal lasted almost three hours.

As we went from the first course to the last one, I became increasingly full. My gracious hostess kept offering me more and more food. But I just couldn't keep going.

Finally, in an effort to tell her I'd had all I could eat, I pulled together the three French words I remembered that would tell her I was full. "*Je suis plein*," I said, which literally translates to "I am full." I was quite proud of myself for being able to connect a few words for a cogent sentence in French that would be easily understood.

A moment of silence ensued. A few people exchanged quick glances and a few muffled snickers. Then everyone in the room broke out into uproarious laughter. It continued for a couple of minutes. One of my teammates grabbed my arm and his side at the same time, consumed in a belly laugh, tears pouring down his face. I was perplexed, the only person in the room who didn't understand what evidently had been a very funny joke.

Here was the problem: At that point in my French immersion, I didn't yet understand idioms. All languages have them, including English. In French, *je suis plein* is one of them. Literally translated, it does mean "I am full." But as a French idiom, it means "I am pregnant."

Can you imagine my enormous embarrassment when one of my teammates, in English, told me my faux pas? My hostess had asked if I wanted more food. Essentially I had responded, "No thank you; I'm pregnant."

I wanted to hide under the table. But my hosts were extremely gracious and understanding. They assured me they'd heard this kind of mistake in translation before. Eventually I was able to laugh about it as well. Unfortunately, it was not the last time I'd make such an error. But my new friends always corrected me with kindness. In time, I was able to master the idioms.

I grew to love my new friends and their culture—especially the food. It makes me hungry whenever I remember the delicious French food—especially that memorable seven-course meal (in spite of my unfortunate, memorable mistake!).

The basketball part of my life in Nice became especially enjoyable. The team I played on melded into a strong unit. We played well together and were quite formidable.

At one point we received an invitation to play in a three-day tournament in Yugoslavia (before it became present-day Serbia). Basketball is hugely popular in this part of the world. Some of the best teams from all over Europe came to participate. The stands were packed with rabid basketball fans supporting the different teams.

For three days, I had one of those tournaments every player who has ever played the game dreams about. For three straight games, I could do no wrong. I could have drop-kicked the basketball and it still would have gone in the basket.

From the opening second of the first game, my teammates sensed how well I was playing. They constantly fed me the ball. No matter where I was on the court, they tried to find me and pass the ball to me. And I didn't let them down. For all three days, no one could stop me. The opponents tried everything to slow me down—from double-teaming me to a box-and-one defense to trick-and-gimmick defenses. Nothing succeeded.

We won the tournament. After its completion, all the teams encircled the edge of the court. The director of the tournament gave the third-place team their trophy, then awarded the second-place team their trophy. Then the announcer called out the winner of the tournament: the team from Nice, France. A loud ovation followed. All the players from my team went forward to accept the trophy. It was a special moment.

Then we went back to our place at the edge of the court. The announcer continued with his script. I didn't understand a word he was saying. Finally, the fans in the stands broke out into a loud applause, as did all the players on the opposing teams. I started applauding as well, not knowing exactly what was going on, but politely trying to fit in with everyone else.

My teammates started surrounding me. They took me by my elbows, slapped me on the back, rubbed my hair, and ushered me back to the trophy platform. I didn't realize that the announcer had just called out my name as the winner of the Most Valuable Player award! He presented me with a huge, shiny silver trophy. The applause lasted for several more minutes. Chills danced down my back.

It was one of the most meaningful, memorable moments of my life. I had never played like that before or ever again. But for a few moments, I played the game of basketball at the highest level possible for me.

For years thereafter, that trophy was always put in a place of prominence wherever I lived—while I was in graduate school at the University of Florida (where I worked as a graduate assistant basketball coach after finishing my stint in Europe playing basketball), and while I was in seminary afterward. The trophy held a special memory for me. It represented the pinnacle of accomplishment in a sport where I'd spent countless hours honing my skills and ability.

Then I met Marilynn. We fell in love and married, moved to Charlotte, and bought our first home. The trophy was put in a closet. Seven years later, we moved into our second home, where we have remained to this day.

The writing of this book revealed to me the fact that the word *honor* can refer to a prize or trophy. That, in turn, led me to think that when a husband honors his wife, he will view her as his once-and-for-all trophy bride.

How does this connect with the basketball trophy that I won in Yugoslavia decades ago? I think it does in two ways.

First, remembering this trophy forced me to ask myself, *Where is it now?* Guess what? I can't remember! I think it's in our attic. But I'm not entirely sure. It's tucked away somewhere among other items from my past. No longer does it have a place of prominence in my life. No longer is it considered extraordinarily special in my home. It's gathering dust in my attic along with other not-so-special pieces of memorabilia from long ago.

Second, it forced me to ask, *What would I consider my most precious trophy now?* The answer to this question came quickly and easily. All

I had to do was look around my house and office to see what is most prominently on display.

When someone enters these places, what would he see first and foremost? Pictures of my three kids (and my grandkids) sprinkled everywhere. I'm very proud of them all. They hold a special place in my heart. They are all true treasures to me.

But even more prominently on display are pictures of Marilynn. They range from when we were on our honeymoon, to vacation times together through the years, to mission trips we shared together, to simple photos of her at different ages and stages of her life. They serve as constant reminders of this amazing woman and life partner who has stood by me in times of ministry crisis; held my forehead in the middle of the night as I vomited and then nursed me back to health; mothered and nurtured all three of our kids; and put up with my gross sinfulness, arrogance, and pride.

She is my special trophy. She is what I prize most in the world. She deserves the places of foremost prominence in my life.

Husband, it's great to enjoy trophies that are a testament to your earthly successes. There is nothing wrong with feeling pride in a job well done. It's okay to display your awards. But they are fleeting. They fade in importance as the years go by. They often end up stuffed in a closet gathering dust.

Why not choose a different course and make your wife your trophy? Put pictures of her everywhere you spend a lot of time—in your home, your car, and your office. Where possible, create a panorama of pictures of your life together. Then glance at pictures frequently throughout the day and thank God for giving you this special trophy. The photos of your wife will serve as constant reminders of God's grace. They will also help keep you focused on what you consider most important in life.

Your kids will notice (as will your grandkids). In doing this, you will plant seeds in their hearts about what's the most valuable kind of trophy in life.

And when you are on the road and could be tempted to be disloyal to your wife, either in response to flirtations from another woman or by watching something you shouldn't on the motel's television, put a picture of her on top of the television set. Every time you look at what's on the screen, you will see her. You'll be reminded that you've made a covenant with your eyes (Job 31:1). You'll remember what a glorious, valuable trophy she is. You'll think about all the hard work you've already put into your marriage to make it work. You'll remember the kids you've both helped birth and given life to.

You'd dare not do anything to hurt your wife's heart. She is too valuable to you. She's your esteemed, valued, respected trophy.

Your relationship with your permanent trophy bride will never be stuffed into a cobwebbed corner in your attic, becoming duller by the day, gathering layers of dust as the years go by. To the contrary! It will glow ever brighter with the passage of time.

And you will similarly glow with delight in your heart at what this trophy really means to you.

The two of you have truly become one.

You will hear the standing ovation of those in heaven.

What else in life could be more valuable?

7

Be a Guardian and Gardener

I RECENTLY WAS ASKED to speak at a memorial service for fallen police officers. Those present included active and retired officers, politicians, and family members of officers who had been killed in the line of duty. I felt honored to speak to them.

What did I say?

I spoke to them about the call from God upon their lives as police officers. Their work is not merely an occupation, something that takes up their time for eight-plus hours a day. It is much more a vocation, the same word from which we get *voice*. It's God's voice to their ears, a true calling from him to them, for his will to be done through them here on earth.

This calling from God has a twofold purpose. First, it's a call to protect citizens from evil. Biblically, police officers are instruments of God's wrath against lawless people to administer his justice on this side of eternity (Romans 13:1-7). When bad guys try to kill, steal, or destroy, police officers are the first people we summon to the scene.

Second, it's a call to serve citizens in times of distress and trouble. We hate to see the red and blue lights swirling and blinking in our rear-view mirror when we've been caught speeding. But we love to see these same lights pulling up behind us when our car is stranded on the road-side because of engine or tire failure. We know they've come to help and serve us in our time of need.

After my message, someone read out loud the names of all the police officers who had paid the ultimate sacrifice. A bell tolled after each name was mentioned. Everyone had a sheet of paper with the officers' names, pictures, background information, and accomplishments. One name went back to 1904!

After all the names had been read, there was a pregnant pause of silence. Then a 21-gun salute crackled through the silence. No other sound could be heard. It was a somber, chilling, thoughtful, penetrating moment to honor those called by God to protect and serve us, and who had given their lives in the line of duty.

I'm not sure why, but during the 21-gun salute, my thoughts immediately raced to husbands and fathers. Perhaps it's because I was writing this book. Or maybe it was simply because I'm concerned that our culture increasingly suggests that husbands and fathers are mere "add-ons," with decreasing significance in marriage and family life.

I found myself thinking God wants more good husbands and fathers—and that husbands and fathers have a vocation similar to police officers: to protect and serve their wives and families. Being a husband and father is not irrelevant. It doesn't occupy our time for only a few hours a week. It's a vocation. It's the greatest possible calling from God. We should even be willing to give our lives in our line of duty.

Plus, it emphatically honors our wives when we gladly accept this responsibility. They inwardly yearn to see us initiate this oversight. It helps oneness occur.

The Husband as Spiritual Leader

In addressing the husband as the spiritual leader of his home, I have no desire to be politically incorrect. Nor do I want to offend women in any way. I don't think I'm a chauvinist. I don't believe it's a man's world.

I've witnessed the terrifying, abusive actions of some husbands who quote the Scripture when they interact with their wives, telling them they are commanded to be submissive to them in every way. These husbands have totally misunderstood God's Word and have used it for their own egotistical, domineering purposes.

Both Marilynn and I are committed to the authority of God's Word. Daily, we try to live in a God-honoring, biblically faithful, love-filled, complementary relationship. Most of the time, we are successful. We know we are created equally in the sight of God. I know Eve was created from Adam's side, not from under his feet (Genesis 2:22). I know in many ways Marilynn is smarter and more gifted than I am. Actually, I'm honored to say that!

God's view of the equality of women was first expressed to Israel's women. Compared to the pagan, cultic peoples around them, God gave Jewish women many rights other cultures didn't allow. They could own property. They were allowed to inherit their father's estates (Numbers 36:1-13).

Though divorce laws were given to Moses (Deuteronomy 24:1-5), the prophet Malachi stated clearly that God hates divorce (Malachi 2:16). The reason he gave these laws was to protect women from destitution and prostitution. He knew that divorce destroyed oneness—his goal for all marriages—and often a woman's personal life.

In the New Testament, we read that a number of women supported Jesus' ministry "out of their means" (Luke 8:1-3). And when Jesus was nailed to the cross, most of his male disciples fled, while many of his women followers stayed to support the one they called "Lord."

When Jesus confronted Martha for chastising Mary's ostensible thoughtlessness in choosing to listen to Jesus instead of helping to serve others, Jesus told Martha that Mary had made the correct choice. Mary was a disciple. She was learning from him as much as possible. As it turned out, she didn't have him much longer. She had chosen wisely. That was the right thing to do. Jesus wanted women to be included among his followers.

It was the women disciples who first discovered the empty tomb and a risen Lord in the early morning hours that fateful Sunday. Jesus' first words spoken as resurrected Lord were to a woman. Isn't that just like God to make women the first witnesses to Jesus' resurrection—in a world that didn't even value women as witnesses? God was making a clear statement: Women are equal participants in his kingdom.

Paul declared all women to be equal citizens in the church. Convincingly he declared the ground at the foot of the cross to be level. All people, both male and female, are equal laborers in the life and ministry of the church (Galatians 3:28). Romans 16 gives a long list of people Paul thanks for helping him in his ministry, many of whom are women.

Yet biblically, men are undeniably called to be the spiritual leaders of their wives and children in the home. The analogy Paul used in Ephesians 5 is that of Jesus and the church. Jesus is the spiritual head of the church. He died to give the church its life. So it should be with the husband. He is called by God to be the spiritual head of his wife and children. He should be willing to die to give his wife and family spiritual life.

Once, in a moment of great love for Marilynn, I said to her, "I love you. I really do. And I'd be willing to die for you." She paused for a moment and responded, "Well, I'm honored that you'd be willing to die for me. I really am. But I think I'd be even more honored if you'd be willing to live for me!"

A husband honors his wife in his willingness to die for her—but especially in his willingness to live for her—and even more especially in the area of spiritual leadership.

Might some husbands misuse and even abuse spiritual leadership? Perhaps. But it's foreign for me to think a husband, filled with the love of Jesus, commanded by his Lord to love his wife and be willing to die for her, would then behave in such an incongruous way. How can you simultaneously love and abuse someone? That makes no sense. It's impossible. It's contrary to common sense.

Therefore, biblically, a husband yearns to obey God's vocation to honor his wife and children by being the spiritual leader of his wife and children. He is called to protect and serve them.

What Spiritual Leadership Looks Like

More practically, what does this mean? More specifically, how can a husband honor his wife as the spiritual leader of his home?

Let me suggest two key ways.

The Husband as a Guardian

In Bible times, for a city to be safe, there needed to be strong walls erected around the city. When an enemy attacked a city, he would first lay siege against the walls. Ramparts would be built so that soldiers could scale the walls. Huge iron hooks would be built to throw over the walls and pull them down. The stronger the walls, the stronger a city would be. Conversely, the weaker the walls, the weaker a city would be.

When the Babylonians captured Jerusalem in 586 BC, they completely razed the walls surrounding the holy city. The Jews were taken into captivity for 70 years. Persia eventually overthrew Babylon and became the world's foremost power. Cyrus, the king of Persia, then allowed some Jews to return home to Jerusalem and the surrounding area.

Building the Walls

Interestingly, many Jews did not return—instead, they stayed behind. One such Jew was named Nehemiah. One day while in prayer, he began to weep. He had a vision of Jerusalem and the people who had returned to their homeland. What caused his tears? He saw his people in a Jerusalem without walls. He knew the people's vulnerability to all enemies and predators. He sensed God's clear call to return and rebuild the walls around Jerusalem.

In the Bible, the book of Nehemiah tells the story of Nehemiah getting permission from Persia's king, Artaxerxes, to rebuild Jerusalem's walls. He returned to Jerusalem to accomplish this call from God. Amidst fierce opposition, he eventually succeeded. The walls around the holy city were rebuilt. The city was now safe again from the exploits of surrounding enemies.

Nehemiah is an example of what husbands should be. We are builders and restorers of the walls around our families. We build them high, wide, and impregnable. We know there is an enemy who wants to destroy marriages and families. He is wily and tireless. He will use an array of different weapons to rob marriages and families of their God-intended purpose.

Therefore, God calls the husband to be aware of the enemy's under-handed, evil tactics. He calls the husband to build strong walls around his home and be the primary guardian against all evil attacks.

Walking the Walls

Psalm 127 is a psalm about the family. It begins, "Unless the LORD builds the house, those who build it labor in vain." The "house" in this verse equals the family. Unless the Lord builds a strong spiritual home, everything else is vanity. If the home flounders, the nation flounders. If the home is destroyed, the nation is destroyed. If the Lord builds strong homes, the nation is strong.

The next line in Psalm 127 says, "Unless the LORD watches over the city, the watchman stays awake in vain" (verse 1). Every strong city has a watchman who walks day and night around the walls. His job is simple: Keep your eyes on the horizon. Note any and all enemy activities. If you see anything, sound the alarm. Take immediate and effective action to protect the city.

If the Lord is building a strong spiritual family, then the husband is like a watchman. He regularly and consistently walks the walls of his family to make sure the evil one's insidious, pernicious plans are not successful. This husband and father is not detached. He is involved in his wife and children's spiritual lives, like a watchman judiciously walking the walls of a city. He's like a guardian carefully overseeing the health of a city.

If you are a husband carefully walking the walls to protect your wife and family, there are specific things you'll know about and examine. What are they?

First, you'll know about your enemy, the devil. He hates your family. He wants to destroy anything you are trying to build for the Lord. Therefore, like a coach preparing to play against and defeat his opponent, he spends countless hours studying your walls. He sees your family's weaknesses. He probes with tireless, tantalizing, and tempestuous temptations—anything that will cause you, your wife, or your kids to fall and fail. He cackles with delight when he ensnares any of you. He wants to render your witness impotent. He will pull no punches to succeed.

Know his schemes. Know his wiles. He is studying you. Study him. Acknowledge his formidability. Realize his strength. Know how he works. Most men are extremely competitive. So be competitive against the evil one. Want him defeated when it comes to your marriage and family.

Begin with yourself. Realize your weaknesses. See places of vulnerability. Know he is probing the walls of your soul, trying to find a weak place where he can tempt you to fail. If he can tempt you to sin, then he knows the first line of defense for your family is gone. Now he can go after your wife and kids.

Be strong in the Lord (Ephesians 6:10). Constantly pray what Jesus taught us to pray: "Lead [me] not into temptation" (Matthew 6:13). In other words, pray that the Holy Spirit will lead you completely away from all the evil one's traps. Flee all immorality (1 Corinthians 6:18). The Lord also knows your weaknesses. Ask him to lead you in the paths of righteousness for his name's sake (Psalm 23:3).

But should you ever succumb to one of the evil one's nefarious snares, immediately ask the Lord to deliver you from the trap. Receive anew his overcoming grace and forgiveness. Rebuild and restore your walls as quickly as possible. And keep fighting!

Next, know your wife's weaknesses. She has them, just as you do. Ask her what she thinks they are. Be in agreement about them. Indelibly etch them in your mind. Regularly and spiritually, walk her walls. Warn her when you see an attack brewing on the horizon. Be her guardian.

And know your kids' weaknesses. Talk with them. Hear their fears. Know their hurts, habits, and hang-ups. Those are the places where the evil one attacks us all. Feel their anxieties. Probe their hearts. Walk their walls. Be their guardian.

You are called to protect them.

The Husband as a Gardener

As the spiritual leader of your home, you are not only a guardian, but also a gardener. Israel was called a vineyard, with God as the vinedresser. His job was to carefully nurture Israel's spiritual life.

The Responsibility of a Gardener

Jesus said that he is the vine, and we who follow him are the branches (John 15:1-2). He talked about how God the Father prunes away anything that is keeping our spiritual lives from fully developing (John 15:2). As the vine, Jesus' job is to nurture our spiritual lives in him. When we live in him, and he lives in us, he produces the fruit of the Spirit in and through us (Galatians 5:22-23).

In the same way that God was a gardener to Israel, so is Jesus to his church. Similarly, husbands should be gardeners who care for their wives and children. They are called by God to spiritually nurture their homes, as God did Israel and Jesus does his church.

What, then, is the primary job of the gardener? Yes, there is a decided defensive aspect to his responsibilities. He is to pluck weeds from the garden. He is to prune what is unnecessary. He is to carefully look for pests and signs of disease. In these ways, he is similar to being a guardian and a watchman who walks the walls of his family's city.

But there is also an overt offensive aspect to his responsibility. He is called to place nutrients in the soil. He is to fertilize the plants. He may even build a greenhouse to ensure the best possible environment. He uses these offensive strategies to give the plants the best chance for survival. The gardener knows that without obstacles and enemies, a fertilized plant will most often grow to full health. It will become what it was intended to be.

Your Priorities as a Gardener

How does a husband serve as a gardener to his wife and family? I believe doing this requires the application of two spiritual nutrients: the Word of God and prayer. The right use of the Bible and intercessory prayer are key to spiritually nourishing a family.

Interestingly, in Acts 6, we read about how the apostles were trying to oversee a new and ever-burgeoning church. People were daily coming to faith in Jesus. Nothing reveals cracks and fissures in an organization like rapid growth. More people bring more problems. More people bring more differing opinions. More people bring more needs.

There arose a conflict between the Jewish and Greek widows. Both needed help from the leaders. What was the apostles' response? Did they try to enter the mess, interact with the two contrary sides, and try to mediate the arguments? No, instead they appointed seven deacons to oversee the problem. These deacons were godly men, filled with the Holy Spirit, who possessed unique gifts of compassion and mercy. They had the skills needed to handle the problem.

What did the apostles then do? The Bible tells us they devoted themselves to the ministry of the Word and prayer (Acts 6:4). They focused on teaching the Bible and involving themselves in intercession. In other words, they assumed the role of gardeners for the early church. They knew their main job was to devote themselves to placing spiritual nutrients in the soil of the garden called the early church.

Notice that when you read about the full armor of God in Ephesians 6—the armor which all followers of Jesus need to defeat the strategies of the evil one—the only two offensive weapons mentioned are the Word of God and intercessory prayer (Ephesians 6:17-18). God's clear instruction for defeating the enemy is to make sure you know and pray God's Word.

The Practice of Nurturing Your Family

How do you apply the nutrients of God's Word and intercessory prayer to your family?

First, you choose to initiate the gardening. This is key. The husband is the one who initiates spiritual oversight. You want to do it! It's a passion in your life, one that's much greater than your passion for your job, sports teams, or other interests.

Husband, it's your responsibility to find the time to talk with your wife about any breaches in her wall. You are to listen intently to her heart and concerns. You are to protect her vulnerabilities and value her insights. Then you are to pray God's Word for her. You are to remind her:

— That no weapon formed against her will prosper (Isaiah 54:17).

— That she is more than a conqueror in Christ Jesus, who loves her (Romans 8:37).

— That the one who lives in her is greater than the one who lives in the world (1 John 4:4).

— That she is not alone in her trials and tribulations. They come to us all. Rain falls on the just and the unjust alike (Matthew 5:45).

— That she needs to rejoice in her tribulation because Jesus has overcome the world (John 16:33).

— That God really loves her through Jesus (John 3:16).

— That nothing can ever separate her from God's love—absolutely nothing (Romans 8:38-39).

— That God promised to meet all her needs according to his riches in Jesus (Philippians 4:19).

— That God is on her side (Psalm 118:6).

— That God is for her (Romans 8:31).

— That there is no condemnation for her because she is in Christ Jesus (Romans 8:1).

— That God is her present help, right now, in her time of trouble and need (Psalm 46:1).

— That God will never leave nor forsake her (Hebrews 13:5).

And the list could go on and on. Someone once purportedly counted all the promises in God's Word and said they totaled 7464. It would do every husband well to get to know the promises that could be claimed and prayed over his wife and the possible places of weakness in her life.

Yes, this assumes that the husband knows how to pray God's Word. As a gardener knows how to use fertilizer, so a husband knows how to pray God's Word. As a soldier knows how to wield a sword, so a husband knows how to pray God's Word. It's not merely optional if you want victory to occur.

In several places in this book, I've noted the need for a husband and wife to have a regular, weekly time together. Here is another way this time should be used. It should be a special, holy Sabbath time where the Word of God can be powerfully prayed over your wife. You can also intercede with God's Word for her throughout the day when you are apart. You can be in a meeting with business associates and silently fertilize her heart with God's Word through prayer. No time or place limits you from doing this.

When you pray God's Word for your wife, you add nutrients to her soul. You build a strong and impregnable wall of defense around her heart—one that spiritually protects her from the enemy. She is stronger spiritually because of it. She feels honored because of it.

And the two of you are drawn closer and closer to God's will for your marriage: oneness.

Then, as spiritual gardener, you should do the same for your children. First, as with your wife, you spend time with them and explore their vulnerabilities. Remember that kids spell love T-I-M-E. You listen to their hearts. If they sense your sincerity, they will tell you their inward angsts. They will share their weaknesses and vulnerabilities with you. What child wouldn't want a father genuinely caring for his eternal soul? Note their heartfelt needs in your mind. List them in a notebook. Be very aware of them.

Then make sure you have regular time with them when you can pray God's Word over them. Probably the most natural time to do so is right before they go to bed. Most often their hearts are open and vulnerable. They are ready for a steady hand and a faith-filled heart to speak spiritual nutrients into their soul before they go to sleep.

You can pray things like:

— The fact Jesus loves children and wants them to come to him (Matthew 19:14).

— God knows each one of us personally by our names (Isaiah 43:1).

— God has his angel armies watching over them day and night (Psalm 91).

— God did not give us a spirit of fear but of love, peace, and a sound mind (2 Timothy 1:7).

— God is good and his mercies endure forever (Psalm 107:1).

— God loves to give good gifts to his children (Matthew 7:11).

— God's plans for them are good and their future is filled with great hope (Jeremiah 29:11).

— Your children are a gift from God and you're delighted to be their dad (Psalm 127:3).

— Your kids should never be afraid because God will never leave nor forsake them (Isaiah 41:10).

— The evil one tries to do his worst to God's children, but God still uses it for good (Genesis 50:20; Romans 8:28).

— God loves to restore what has been taken from us (Isaiah 61:7; Job 42:10).

— Jesus came to give us life and to give it to us abundantly (John 10:10).

— Nothing can ever snatch us from his loving, sovereign hand (John 10:28).

— God loves to lead us beside green grass and still waters to restore our soul (Psalm 23:2-3).

— Jesus will be with us even to the close of time (Matthew 28:20).

This list could go on and on. Pray God's Word over your children. Lay hands on their forehead or their heart while you pray for them. There's great power in physical touch accompanying praying God's Word. Speak life to them. Speak hope to them. Speak blessing to them. Then watch them sleep soundly and securely.

Take the Initiative to Lead

In the course of any given week, the final place where I practiced being a gardener to my family was the Saturday night before Sunday worship. Marilynn and I would gather the kids together. We'd have a Bible lesson to present to them. Sometimes we'd let them act out a Bible story. Their interpretations of what had happened in a Bible story sometimes bordered on the hilarious.

Their allowance would be ten dimes. The first dime was always given to the church—we were trying to teach them, at an early age, the value and necessity of the tithe. Then I'd ask them for their prayer needs. And I would pray for them. More specifically, I would pray God's Word over them. For example, there was a time when my daughter fought against what we called "fret flies." So I would pray over her verses about being free from fear. I would pray for all three children, Marilynn, and myself in this manner. In every way possible, I tried to create a home where grace was clearly practiced.

My wife and children all saw spiritual leadership as my responsibility. There was no mistake about it: I was my family's spiritual guardian and gardener. And in the same way that a great closing pitcher wants the baseball in the ninth inning with a one-run lead, I wanted this responsibility to be the guardian and gardener of my family's life. I wanted to be the spiritual leader. It was a passionate desire. I knew it couldn't be a secondary afterthought if my family was to be spiritually healthy.

That I did this especially honored Marilynn. She desired for me to take on this responsibility. I gladly did so. Because I did, we were drawn closer together.

As Goes the Family

God has given every husband and father a special vocation. Like a police officer, he is called to protect his family. He is to observantly walk the family's walls and protect all within from the vicious, pernicious, and surreptitious attacks of the enemy. He is to be its guardian.

Also, like a police officer, the husband and father has the call from God to serve. He is to make sure his family's spiritual life is cared for. He needs to make sure proper spiritual nutrients are added regularly to his wife and children's hearts—especially by praying God's powerful Word over his wife and kids. He is to be a gardener.

I'm convinced that somewhere in heaven there is a 21-gun salute crackling in tribute to husbands and fathers who rightly assume and have assumed this responsibility. It's necessary for the spiritual health of the family. And as goes the family, so goes the nation.

Equally important is the fact that when husbands do this, they honor their wives. Their wives' hearts are drawn closer to them.

And most important of all, this makes them one.

HONOR COLLECTIVE MEMORIES

There is a scene in the movie *Titanic* that I've never forgotten. As the ship is going down, most of the people are frantically pushing and shoving their way to the upper deck to enter the few available lifeboats. Everyone's survival depends on getting to the lifeboats.

Everyone, that is, except one elderly married couple. They realize their destiny is determined. They are too old and weak to fight, push, and shove their way to the deck. They can't escape their doom. Their fate is sealed. It's useless to resist. They yield their lives to the inevitability of death.

They are alone in their suite on the boat, nattily attired in the evening garb they were wearing when the ship first struck the iceberg. He is wearing his tuxedo, she her evening gown. Accepting the reality of their hopeless situation, they serenely laid down on the bed. He reached over and grabbed her hand. They both closed their eyes, waiting for the inexorable crash of water that would soon break into their room, sweep over their bodies, and bring certain death.

That's eventually what happened. They died together, gently holding each other's hands. It was an emotionally jarring scene. Two elderly people who cared deeply for one another, their fingers inextricably intertwined. They were doggedly devoted to one another until the last second of their lives.

My conjecture is they were most certainly united as one flesh. They had apparently enjoyed a rich, deep marriage bond for many decades. Even in death, they were one.

When I think about this scene, many questions arise. For example, I ask, "I wonder what their last thoughts were before they drowned? Did they think about their wedding vows at the altar? Or did they reflect upon the births of their children? Or did they remember significant achievements in the lives of their children? Or did they focus on their grandchildren and their births and successes? Or were they simply happy to be together in these last moments before death?"

The movie gives no hint if these questions were even contemplated. All we know is they died hand-in-hand, two lives mysteriously intermixed with complete contentedness.

But these questions are interesting for us to consider, aren't they? If we were in that situation with our spouse, what would go through our mind? What kind of collective memories might flood our souls if we were about to face certain death with our beloved?

There is a fascinating phenomenon in marriage called collective memories. These memories are the stealth superglue that makes two people one. They are the silent cement that intertwines two hearts forever. That's one of the reasons divorce is so dreadful. It not only kills a marriage, ripping apart oneness, but it destroys the couple's collective memories as well. The longer the marriage has lasted, the more collective memories that are destroyed.

Divorce evaporates what two people uniquely share together as one.

For example, there will never again be times when a husband takes his wife's hand and warmly asks, "Do you remember when we met?" Or, "Do you remember when our first child was born?" Or, "Do you remember how hard those first years were and how we didn't think we would make it, but we overcame those obstacles together?" Or, "Do you remember when our son made his first basket? And when our daughter won that award?" Or, "Do you remember when God provided that miracle for us when there seemed to be no answer?"

These moments can no longer be shared together as one flesh.

There will never again be vacation times at the beach with the kids when mom and dad tell a story, laughingly throwing back their heads, joyful tears streaming from their eyes and asking, "Do you remember when this happened?" Then all the kids join in the fun, howling in agreement, correcting details, guffawing over the stories while giving their perspective and insights into what they think really happened. The uproarious jibes and arguments over silly, minute perspectives can last for hours. And everyone's heart is strangely and happily warmed during these unique family times.

Suddenly, with divorce, these collective memories are...*poof*...gone.

No longer are there times when parents, grandparents, and grandkids are all present and the memories gush from the heart. God intended moments like these to be generational exclamation marks. He wanted these stories to be life lessons passed down from grandpa and grandma to grandkids—lessons affirmed by parents, lessons that can be learned only through experience. These moments are priceless. They help build the character, faith, and hope of young grandkids, which will then be passed on to their children and others as well.

Suddenly, they are evaporated in the maelstrom of divorce.

Husband, one of the major reasons to honor your wife and keep moving toward oneness with her is not only to prevent divorce and guard oneness, but to protect the collaborative cargo of collective memories as well. You must guard these memories at all costs. They are priceless, beyond value, for you, your kids, grandkids, and generations to come.

And they devastatingly disappear when divorce occurs.

Shouldn't we husbands do everything possible to divorce-proof our marriages and safeguard the precious cargo of collective memories? Shouldn't we do everything possible to learn how to honor our wives and secure oneness till death do us part?

One tangible way is by remembering and practicing the Five-Year Rule. What is it? It's the belief, rooted in scientific data, that if a couple will just lock the door of their marriage from the outside, saying divorce is simply not an option, and then choose to work through their difficulties, five years later they will be exceedingly glad they did. When this is done, couples describe their marriages as happier than ever. They are exceedingly thankful for what they learned.

What did they learn? From listening to their stories, I hear them talk about how they learned perseverance, forgiveness, and how to work through problems together. They realized that the issues that once loomed overwhelmingly large really weren't that large. They discovered that working through the problems made them stronger individually and collectively. They discovered that if they made it through one tough time, they could do it again...and again...and again!

In choosing to steadfastly work through their marital issues, they are very glad they did. I hear them describe how they now laugh and scoff at what they previously thought were impossible marital problems to overcome.

Most importantly, they safeguarded their collective memories. They now possess a virtual treasure trove of memories that will encourage their kids, grandkids, and others outside their family when their tough times arrive. They encourage others to believe that nothing is impossible with God. They are able to tell others that all marital wounds can be healed and huge rifts bridged by God's great grace.

If you want to honor your wife, practice the Five-Year Rule. No matter what obstacle you may be facing in your marriage, believe it will be different five years from now. Persevere through the tough times. Work with your beloved on your issues. Keep talking. Keep forgiving. Keep giving grace to the other.

After the five years are over, see if your marriage isn't better and stronger. See if your problems aren't significantly smaller.

And rejoice over all the incomparable collective memories you've been able to safeguard for your kids, your grandkids, and future generations.

In doing so, I can only imagine that the elderly couple in the movie *Titanic* would pat you on the back for a job well done.

8

Use Words Wisely

"THOSE ARE JUST WORDS," people sometimes say dismissively. They are trying to state how unimportant another person's perspective or opinion is. They are saying words don't really matter.

But they are wrong. Dead wrong. Words are important. They were God's idea. He invented words. They come from his heart. They express ideas, feelings, and insights. Try having an intimate, meaningful human relationship without words. It's impossible. Even the hearing-impaired have hand signals—a way to "hear" and express words from and to another.

When God wanted to show his character, "the Word became flesh and dwelt among us" (John 1:14). He incarnated "the Word" to express himself to our world.

Words can inflame. People have used words to slander others and cause enormous personal harm to them. History shows that before you can commit genocide you must negatively caricature people, even entire ethnic groups, with negative words.

"Sticks and stones may break my bones, but words will never hurt me" simply isn't true. It may seem like a clever phrase to utter in a moment of ostensible courage. But it's simply not true. In fact, it's a lie. Words do hurt. Some people, even all the way into adulthood, are indelibly scarred by vicious, pernicious words spoken to them as children. They still hear egregiously painful words from parents, teachers, coaches or significant others—words like, "You'll never amount to anything. Why can't you be like _____?"

It is written in Proverbs 18:21, "Death and life are in the power of the tongue." What wisdom! Words give either life or death.

Proverbs 15:1 says, "A soft answer turns away wrath, but a harsh word stirs up anger." One single word can prevent or cause all kinds of negative or positive emotions to occur.

Jesus had this to say about our words in Matthew 12:36: "I tell you, on the day of judgment people will give account for every careless word they speak, for by your words you will be justified, and by your words you will be condemned." Jesus knew that a person's words reflect their inner character, which will be revealed on judgment day.

In James 3, the writer points out the extraordinary danger of words spoken from the tongue. Words can be like a tiny spark that sets an entire forest ablaze. Humanity has been able to bridle the strongest animals on earth, but not this tiny instrument in our mouths called the tongue. From it, sometimes simultaneously, pours forth praises to God and criticisms of people he created in his image. How incongruous!

Can any thinking person deny the power of words? I don't think so.

Words for a Famous Musician

During the tumultuous 1960s, many public schools faced the daunting task of integration. No place was more tumultuous than Detroit, Michigan. Racial tensions consumed this proud city.

Mrs. Beneduci was an elementary school teacher in Detroit during these days. Affirming the need for integration and her belief that all people are created equal in the sight of God, she welcomed the new African-American students in her classroom.

However, one child's assimilation into his new environment proved particularly difficult and challenging. His name was Stephen Morris, a diminutive nine-year-old. He seldom spoke. He was not only black, but also sight-impaired. How could she get the other children to accept him?

One day Mrs. Beneduci came up with an ingenious idea. She hid the class's pet mouse in the wastepaper basket. Then in the middle of one of her lectures, she turned around and noted that the mouse was out of its cage. The children's responses ranged from laughter to a few girls fearfully climbing on their chairs.

Mrs. Beneduci asked all the kids to settle down. She said they really needed to find the mouse. Then she turned to Stephen Morris. She noted his exceptional hearing ability. So she asked Stephen if he would listen intently and find the mouse.

Stephen first asked the class for total silence. After a few moments, he correctly determined the class mouse was in the wastepaper basket. He was quite proud of himself.

Then Mrs. Beneduci flooded Stephen's soul with life-giving words. She told him what a wonderful gift of hearing he had been given. She concluded her cascade of encouragement by saying, "Stephen Morris, you are a wonder!"

Thereafter, his classmates nicknamed him "Little Stevie Wonder."

Within months, Stevie began to explore his hearing gift. This unearthed an extraordinary musical giftedness. Some time later he recorded the first of many gold records, "Fingertips Part II."

Think about it. The entire history of American rock 'n' roll and rhythm and blues was dramatically transformed because an elementary school teacher used her words wisely—words that helped unlock Stevie Wonder's wondrous musical gifts!

I love to share this story. Once, when speaking in Detroit, I shared it. Everyone, as usual, appreciated it. Afterward, a young man approached me. He told me how much he enjoyed my talk. Then he said, "About that Mrs. Beneduci story..."

Uh, oh! I thought to myself. *I'm in Detroit, Michigan. Maybe I messed up the story!* Every speaker's nightmare is to tell a story wrong or give misinformation.

The young man continued, "I'm her grandson!" Gulp. Immediately I asked him if I got the story right.

"Oh yes," he responded. "You got it all correct. But let me tell you the rest of the story."

He then went on to tell me that Stevie Wonder and his grandmother became lifelong friends. They stayed in touch regularly. In fact, at the celebration of the entrance of the twenty-first century in Detroit, the city leaders asked Stevie Wonder to return and do a huge downtown concert for the entire city. He agreed, but with one caveat. Mrs. Beneduci must be on the platform with him, and they must be granted a few moments together to speak to the city.

The organizers readily agreed. At the concert, there on the platform were Stevie Wonder and Mrs. Beneduci. When they spoke together, they pleaded with the citizens of Detroit to put aside racial prejudices and work together as one.

Finally, Mrs. Beneduci's grandson told me how profoundly she had affected his life. He had five children, two who were his own and three who were adopted. The three adopted children were African-American. His grandmother's love for African-American children had inspired the adoptions.

Mrs. Beneduci changed lives because she used her words wisely. It could even be argued she changed the world because of her words.

USING WORDS WISELY IN MARRIAGE

If using words wisely is important in every sphere of life, how much more important is it for husbands to use words wisely in the marriage relationship? First Peter 3:7 says, "Likewise, husbands, live with your wives in an understanding way, showing honor to the woman as the weaker vessel, since they are heirs with you of the grace of life, so that your prayers may not be hindered." If my job description as a husband includes honoring my wife so my prayers will be answered, then it's imperative I learn how to honor Marilynn with my words.

Over the many years we have been married, I've said things that have honored her. Her soul has been enriched when I've done this. Sadly, I've also said things that have dishonored her. Her soul has withered when I've done this. Life and death truly is in the tongue!

Therefore, from my personal experience with my wife, let me share with you some phrases that I've learned honor her well. They have made her smile and warmed her heart. Most importantly, they have moved our hearts toward one another.

"I'm honored to be your husband."

I once said this in a sermon. It wasn't frivolous, nor was it frothy. It wasn't used for effect. I meant every word of it. I wanted my listeners to know how much I prize Marilynn as my wife. I wanted them to know that she is my true, one-and-only, forever "trophy bride."

I was amazed at how many women commented to me how much they appreciated the way I publicly honored Marilynn. I readily sensed there was a hunger in their hearts for their husbands to do the same. I knew I had unearthed a verbal treasure that I needed to do more with Marilynn personally and privately—and encourage husbands to follow suit.

I once wrote a note to Marilynn. I didn't think it to be a particularly big deal. I simply told her how honored I was to be her husband. I left it in the kitchen before I went to work. It was soon taped to the refrigerator. It remained there for several years. An added benefit was that the kids saw it every day when they opened the refrigerator door.

My counsel to husbands is specific. Tell your wife you are honored to be her husband. Say this publicly and privately, frequently, and without hesitation. Look for every opportunity to say it. At times, she may become a bit embarrassed. But she will also beam inwardly with joy.

"I love you more than you love me."

Okay, this may seem a bit competitive and silly. But it's turned into a fun game on my part. Often I'll enter the room where Marilynn is and say, "You know, honey, I am absolutely convinced that I love you more than you love me." She always smiles and dismissively waves me off. But she always smiles.

In fact, in bed, right before we go to sleep, often I'll recount the evening with her. Then I'll say something like, "And you know that restaurant we went to tonight? Well, right before we left the waiter took me aside and said he was very concerned for our marriage. He said that throughout the serving of the meal it was obvious to him that I loved you more than you loved me."

Marilynn always giggles and says, "Oh David, let's go to sleep." We do. But I am certain her soul feels honored by my little competitive joke.

And I'm also convinced she sleeps a bit better because of it. It's a wise way to use a trite phrase.

"Thank you for all you do for me."

Marilynn does a lot for me. I could not live the life I live if she didn't live the life she lives. She has chosen to do the books so I don't have to. She has created a home for me that is a refuge from a very busy pastoral schedule. It doesn't go unnoticed by me. I know that if I'm successful at all in my life, it's largely because of the sacrifices Marilynn Chadwick makes for me.

One Mother's Day, I decided to tell her this in a public way. I asked my worship team if they could have the offertory be Huey Lewis and the News' song "Doing It All for My Baby." The final line of the chorus says how happy this man is for all the things his girl does for him. Everyone enjoyed our rendition of the song. But I think everyone especially enjoyed it when I got up on the platform and said, "That was a great song. I asked the worship band to do it. I wanted to honor my wife Marilynn—for everything she has done for me."

Then came applause. Then came Marilynn's bit of embarrassment. Then, at home, came the smile—that wonderful smile that I fell in love with. She thanked me for all I've done for her too. It was a special moment in our marriage.

Husband, try to say this phrase repeatedly to your wife. If you ever have the opportunity, say it publicly. Just say it! My bet is, as in my case, your wife does far more for you than you ever realize.

Let her know you're trying to realize it!

"I never want to take you for granted."

These wise words naturally follow "Thank you for all you do for me."

If you begin to notice all that your wife does for you, then you won't take her for granted.

I remember a time when Marilynn and I had an intense disagreement (that's a polite term for a fight!). I can't remember what it was about. Do we ever much remember? It was most assuredly over something silly that eventually escalated. Anyway, it was something that hurt her heart and caused a tit-for-tat between us.

When things finally settled down, she said to me, "I just don't want you to take me for granted." It became exceedingly apparent to me that this was the issue behind the issue. She felt I'd done it more than once. And I'd done it again. It was extremely important to her that I understand she felt that I had taken her for granted, and she didn't like it.

I knew I needed to change. I intentionally started to look for ways she serves me. I started noticing every meal she fixes for me, when she picks up my clothes from the drycleaners, and when she brings me a cup of tea in the morning while I'm studying and praying. I especially began to notice the way she faithfully loved and cared for our kids (and now grandkids!).

The more I looked, the more I discovered the countless ways Marilynn cared for me. Many of these acts of kindness were small. But added up over a long period of time, it became obvious how much she gave to me.

After noticing more of what Marilynn did, I became much more purposeful in thanking her for doing them. I constantly thank her by giving her verbal affirmations for the ways she serves me. And I end the "thank you" with "I never want to take you for granted."

It's another way to use words wisely!

"I'm never leaving you."

Nearly four decades ago I made vows to Marilynn. I said things that any sane man would think through seriously before speaking. Primarily, I said I'm marrying forever. No matter what the feelings or circumstances may be, I'm staying. In sickness or in health, I am staying. In good times or in bad, I'm staying. In plenty and in want, I'm staying.

In joy and in sorrow, I'm staying. I'm choosing, for the rest of my life, to forsake all others. I've made these covenant promises to her for the glory of God.

I meant every word of these vows. Here's my question: Why not reassure her over and over again? Why not let her know, "I'm never leaving you. Never!"

It's not that Marilynn worries about me leaving. She inherently knows I never will. She knows how seriously I take my vows and that I'm staying no matter what. But for her to hear of my commitment honors her. It reassures her of my love for her. It gives her security in an insecure world.

Plus, it's just fun to say and watch her smile in response to these wise words!

"I got the better end of the deal."

Author Marcus Buckingham did a study of successful marriages. He concluded that the most successful marriages were two people who each believe they married beyond themselves. They are two people, in football jargon, who both think they have outrun their coverage. Each partner is convinced he or she got the better end of the deal.

Husband, if you feel that way about your wife, make sure you tell her.

I know I feel that way about Marilynn. I am certain I married well above myself. I stand daily in awe of that fact. Therefore, I regularly say to her, "I'm the lucky one in the marriage." I really do believe that!

She smiles whenever I say it. And have I told you that I love to see her smile?

"Thank you for saying yes."

This is the natural follow up to "I got the better end of the deal." Long ago, my parents taught me the following children's song: "There are two little magic words that can open any door with ease. One little word is thanks and the other little word is please." They used the song to teach me the importance of saying thank you frequently to others.

Therefore, I say thank you regularly to Marilynn for agreeing to marry me. She didn't have to say yes. There were other suitors. But she said yes to me. How amazing!

It has now become a game between us—when I say, "Thanks for marrying me," she always responds with, "Thanks for asking!"

Then she smiles. The smile alone is worth speaking these wise words.

"I am a better man because of you."

This is the ultimate compliment. I believe most women enter marriage hoping they can help their husbands become all God wants them to be. Marilynn has certainly done that for me. Everything she is and all she has done has allowed me to become who I am and achieve what I've achieved.

We stated this same basic thought a bit earlier. But here, it's nuanced a bit differently. When I say, "I am a better man because of you," I am acknowledging my sin when I entered the marriage relationship and how God used my wife to shave off those rough edges, to give me insights into my prideful, selfish, sinful nature and yet still be loved.

It's clearly saying, "While I was still a gross sinner, you chose to love me unconditionally. You chose to give me grace I didn't deserve. And for that, I'm eternally grateful. I'm a better man because of your unconditional acceptance of me."

You've probably heard the saying that we stand on the shoulders of those who have gone before us. That is, if we are successful, it's because someone helped us to be successful. For me, that person is largely my wife Marilynn. I bet that's true for you with regard to your wife as well.

If so, tell your wife that you are a better man because of her! Honor her by telling her you know it's true. It will enlarge your persona in her eyes.

"I'm praying for you."

Do you know that your wife inwardly hungers to be married to a man seeking after God's own heart? Do you know that deep down she yearns for someone who shares her heart for God and spiritual truths? Do you know that she wants you to be her prayer partner?

If I'm right and she wants to pray with you, here's a way to use your words wisely to let her know your heart for her and your heart for prayer. Ask about her needs, and tell her you're praying for her. Send her a text or e-mail mentioning the prayer needs that she shared with you. Or maybe send a tweet. Or leave a voice message. Or leave a note on her pillow. Even snail mail will work! Just let her know that you are praying for her throughout the day. She will be overjoyed to know that her life partner is remembering to take her to God's throne of grace through prayer, asking God to help her.

Then make sure you really do pray for her. Don't be disingenuous. Prayer must be important to you. Then you'll want to make it important for you and your wife together. You'll make an effort to find a time when you can pray together regularly. She'll be deeply appreciative. It will meld your hearts together more as one in Christ.

You honor your wife's heart for the Lord as you use your words wisely in prayer.

Use Post-It Notes

Okay, this isn't a verbal affirmation. But I think you'll get the point.

On one of Marilynn's birthdays, I was trying to think of a new way to say, "I love and appreciate you." I wanted to avoid the "same ol' same ol'" when it came to celebrating her birthday. You know: cards, cake, dinner, balloons, etc. Those are fine. I just felt, "Been there, done that."

So on the day of her birthday, after she had left the house to run an errand, I came home from work. I wrote out dozens upon dozens of little love notes on Post-it papers. On many I wrote the words I'm advising you to say here. I put them all over the house. They were on the television screen. They were in her drawers, on her books, inside her Bible, and on her computer. They were anywhere and everywhere. They proliferated like rabbits.

She didn't find them all on her birthday. She found more over the next several days. But she found enough of them on her birthday to make it special.

They made her smile. And I smiled when I saw her smile.

But do you want to know what's most special? That birthday was several years ago. There are still about six of those Post-it notes in the bedroom. Marilynn has purposefully left them there. Do you think they mean something to her? Do you think she enjoys reading them over and over again?

Written words count. Use them wisely too.

"I'm sorry. Please forgive me."

These are perhaps the hardest words for a man to speak. Perhaps it's that insidious, malevolent, malignant male ego that gets in the way. Perhaps it's human pride. Whatever the source, it needs to be killed, crucified, and obliterated. It's evil and wicked. It has caused more hurt in the world generally and in marriage particularly than anything else.

That's been the case in my marriage. I spent some time on the subject in a previous section in the book. But let me restate it: I've probably hurt Marilynn the most in my disastrous need to be right. There have been times when I've sacrificed her well-being for my need to win the argument and maintain my strange sense of self-righteousness.

When we argue, our oneness is strained. Perhaps, for a moment, it's separated. Answered prayer becomes inhibited (1 Peter 3:7). We are no longer connected together as God desires.

When hurt, husbands especially close off their hearts in anger and retreat into personal, deep caves and harden their feelings. When this has happened in my marriage, I need to admit my heart becomes recalcitrant and I refuse to move toward Marilynn.

That's sin. It's not God's will. The pathway toward restored intimacy is through the wise words, spoken honestly from the heart, that say, "I'm sorry. Please forgive me." Do it. Do it often. Even if you think most of the guilt or blame belongs to your wife. Who the guilt belongs to is not the issue. The real issue is oneness. The goal is to be intimately connected as God desires.

And apologize in front of the children, if necessary. Model for them how to do the same thing in their marriages. Plus, it gives them security when they see mom and dad are okay after an argument and divorce is not going to happen.

We husbands fear that by saying, "I'm sorry" our wives will lose respect for us. To the contrary! They will most often deeply appreciate the humility. Indeed, as the Bible promises, as you humble yourself before the Lord, he will lift you up (James 4:10). And your wife gets to go along for the ride!

I've even had some wives tell me that they fall in love with their husbands again when they humbly say, "I'm sorry. Please forgive me." That is, after the wives have gotten up from the floor in amazement and surprise.

I also believe your willingness to speak these words increases intimacy in the bedroom. Why? Because they open the door for you to become one again. And sexual intimacy is the expression of oneness. You are reconnected together. Remember, Jesus said that God's will in marriage is for two to become one (Matthew 19:6).

When you have two different people, with two different genders, with two different life experiences, with two different genetic codes, brought together in a marriage relationship, you will bump! The question is not *if* you will bump, but *what will you do* when the bumps occur? If you allow the bumps to expose your selfishness and then seek forgiveness, you'll be drawn back together again.

Just make sure the bumps don't become boulders. How can this be prevented? Owning up to your part of the problem, taking the initiative to pursue your wife, and having the courage to say, "I'm sorry. Please forgive me." Then the boulders will be removed from your pathway to intimacy.

They are especially wise words that will especially honor your wife—if you are wise enough to use them!

Final Thoughts

Words are powerful instruments. They express thoughts and feelings. They can build up or tear down someone's self-esteem. They can encourage or discourage. They can motivate or paralyze. They even can move the hand of God in prayer.

Therefore, handle them with care. Use them wisely. In your marriage, use them to draw you closer together and make you one.

And let this be your unceasing prayer that you passionately pursue: "Let the words of my mouth and the meditation of my heart be acceptable in your sight, O LORD, my rock and my redeemer" (Psalm 19:14).

WISE WORDS FROM PRESIDENT CARTER

Jimmy Carter, the 39th president of the United States, is a good and honorable man. Whatever you may believe about his politics and effectiveness as president, it's undeniable that he is a caring human being and has had a positive impact on humanity—especially among the poor.

President Carter's incessant work for the betterment of others was recently brought to the public's attention by the revelation that he had brain cancer. When people reflected upon his life and heard anew all that he had accomplished for others, they were amazed. And admiration for him greatly increased.

For example, he had worked tirelessly for world peace since he left the presidency in 1980, which earned him the Nobel Peace Prize in 2002. At 90+ years of age, he continues to take up a hammer and nails to build houses for the homeless through Habitat for Humanity all over the world. Through the Carter Center in Atlanta, he has worked incessantly to help find cures for diseases, such as river blindness in south Sudan.

President Carter is also faithful to teach his Sunday school class every week in his church in Plains, Georgia. He hates to miss the class when he has to travel. In fact, after the announcement that he had brain cancer, more than 700 people showed up to hear his teaching. He reminded his listeners to put their trust in God alone. In doing so, they could face anything in life.

And President Carter loves his wife. He really, really loves Rosalynn. They married July 7, 1946. They have remained married for almost 70 years. That's an amazing accomplishment within itself. President Carter described their life together as "a life full of love." They truly appear to be one flesh.

President Carter said that early in their marriage he made several decisions without consulting his wife, including leaving the Navy and running for the Georgia Senate. "I learned soon after that that was the wrong approach. But since then, she's been a full and precious and vital partner with me in all that I've done."[1]

He repeatedly and publicly says that the best decision he ever made in life was marrying Rosalynn. He follows this by saying that the happiest day in his life was when he married her. Talk about using words wisely!

When asked to give marriage tips, President Carter counsels all couples to never go to sleep without resolving issues between them. He says, "Just being able to admit you *might* be mistaken and that the other person *might* be right" will greatly enhance your relationship.

After President Carter's brain cancer was revealed, Mark Davis wrote an article about him that appeared in the *Charlotte Observer* on August 24, 2015, entitled, "Jimmy Carter, one of us." Davis shared about a personal experience he had with the former president.

Davis and his new bride were leaving for their honeymoon. The plane was about to take off. It pulled away from the ramp. He and his wife were excited to begin their trip to their honeymoon destination.

Suddenly, the plane came to a complete stop. The engines were shut down. Everyone on board the plane was asking, "What in the world is going on?"

Two dark SUVs appeared from nowhere. The plane's door was opened. Two Secret Service agents entered—dark suits, sunglasses, earpieces and all. They walked down the aisle of the plane, glancing at every passenger in the eyes and making sure all passed their inspection and expectations.

They left. Who then walked on the plane? President Jimmy Carter. As he did so often, he shook hands with several of the passengers until he found his seat. One of those passengers was Mark Davis, the author of the article.

Fifteen years later, Davis was interviewing President Carter on the complexities surrounding the Palestinian Authority. He brought up what happened on the plane. He shared how he was going on his honeymoon and at first blush, when the plane was forced to stop, he was concerned the flight was going to be canceled, thus disrupting all the plans he had carefully made with his new bride.

President Carter laughed and said he remembered that day well. The last thing he would have ever wanted to do was to interrupt a young couple's plans for a glorious honeymoon. Then he turned to the reporter, his eyes becoming much more serious. He asked, "Are you still married?" The reporter proudly responded yes.

"Good," President Carter said. "Stay that way."

It was plain talk from a plain man from Plains, Georgia.

President Carter knows the importance of two becoming one in marriage and that staying such is God's desire for all marriages. And he knows one of the key ways to keep a marriage together is to use words wisely.

One example of this is how President Carter and Rosalynn regularly say "ILYTG" to one another. He started saying it to her when he first became smitten with her at the United States Naval Academy, where he was a cadet. It means, "I love you the goodest." President Carter's mom and dad used to say it to each other regularly. "I picked it up with Rosa," he said.

President Carter had "ILYTG" inscribed on a compact that he gave to Rosalynn years ago. He wanted a way for him to say this phrase to her every day when they were apart. This compact is now on display at the Jimmy Carter Presidential Library in Atlanta. Their kids have carried on this tradition with their mom and dad via emails, texts, and

Twitter. They say it to their spouses as well. I would imagine it's being passed down to their kids and grandkids for generations to come.

I am convinced that one of the reasons President Carter and Rosalynn have enjoyed almost 70 long, fruitful, faithful, meaningful, and joyous years of marriage is because he had learned to use his words wisely with his beloved. They have said "ILYTG" repeatedly to one another all through their marriage.

Pause for a moment now and think about what President Carter said about his beloved—specifically the following two statements. First, the wisest decision he ever made was to marry her. Second, the happiest day of his life was when he married her. And he wants other couples to know and experience these same truths.

You know he speaks these words to her over and over again. You know it is a regular part of his communication habits.

Can you imagine what positive feelings flood Rosalynn's heart when she hears her husband express these sentiments? Do you think it increases her love for him? Do you think more intimacy occurrs between them after he speaks these words? Do you think their hearts increasingly became one as they continued to speak these words over the course of 70 years of marriage? Do you think she desires more and more to honor him?

I'm certain that all this—and more—has happened between them. Jimmy and Rosalynn's marriage is an example to all for what God wills in marriage.

Husband, realize that life and death is rooted in what you say (Proverbs 18:21). Your words either build up or tear down your marriage. They can encourage or discourage your beloved. They can either give hope or despair to your wife. They can motivate or deflate your bride.

Are you building up your wife with your words? Say "ILYTG" ("I love you the goodest") regularly to her. Or come up with another acronym that you can use to affirm one another—like IATLO—"I am the lucky one," or ILYMTLI—"I love you more than life itself."

Let your wife know the best day in your life was when you married her. Tell her every day how much you love her and are honored to be her husband. Let her know without hesitation that you'd unequivocally marry her again.

Use your words wisely with her.

President Jimmy Carter has done that with Rosalynn.

He is a good role model for all us husbands.

EPILOGUE:

Honor in Action

MY MOM AND DAD were born and grew up in Winston-Salem, North Carolina. They came from loving, caring, committed Christian homes. Sadly, both lost a parent earlier than expected or desired.

Dad lost his mom at the tender age of 12. They were extremely close. The loss was terribly traumatic for him. Dad's mom was the one who planted the initial seeds of faith into his heart. She taught him Scripture. She sang the great hymns of the faith over him as he fell asleep at night. Their hearts were joined together in a unique mom/son relationship. Dad always spoke about her with the deepest affection.

He loved to share with me this story. As a young boy, he would awaken in the middle of the night to his mom singing. He would walk to the top of the stairs and glance into the living room, and see her doing what she loved to call her "happy dancing." She danced around the floor, her hands lifted high, singing her songs of praise to the Lord. I'm convinced my dad's deep affection for sacred music was rooted in what he heard and saw from his mom.

You can easily see why her sudden death was devestatingly difficult for him.

My mom lost her dad when he was only 39 years old. He died from a gum disease that could have been easily cured if penicillin had been available. Sadly, it was unavailable, placed on the market just a few months after he passed away.

Mom's dad was a good and honorable man. He loved his family deeply and worked hard to provide for their basic needs. He sincerely loved his wife, Elsie. Mom would regularly tell us how much her heart hurt when she first learned that her father had died.

The Great Depression significantly influenced both my mom and dad and their respective families. Mom's family was not as dramatically impacted as Dad's was. Her dad worked as a train conductor, which was a relatively steady and secure government job. They didn't miss any meals. Most of their needs were supplied. But they still had to work hard and be extremely careful with expenditures.

Dad's family situation was entirely different. When the Great Depression hit, he was ten years old. His mom was still alive. Then, two years into the Depression, his mom passed away. His dad was unemployed. Times were already challenging. And the death of his mom only exacerbated an already-difficult life scenario.

Dad often described in detail the many times when they had little to nothing to eat. His father would look daily for jobs and most often come home having found nothing. He provided what he could, but it wasn't much. He was a single dad, trying to make ends meet and care for his two sons as best he could. Life was challenging for this family of three.

Extreme frugality was practiced regularly, becoming a lifelong part of Dad's mental acumen. The memories of having little haunted Dad's memory into adulthood. I used to tease Dad that he squeezed a nickel so tightly that he made the buffalo on the coin scream in pain! But when you understood where he came from and what his family experienced, it was easy to appreciate his frugality.

A strong work ethic also encompassed much of Dad's upbringing. He would attend school, then immediately come home to do chores. He had to help care for the family. Everything else was secondary.

For example, Dad was a gifted athlete. I am sure my own athletic giftedness came from him. He loved all kinds of sports. But he was never able to develop his gifts in this area. His dad told him he couldn't participate in sports because he needed to come home and do his chores. The family needed him. There simply wasn't enough time in the day for him to do school, sports, and chores. Daily schoolwork and chores took precedence.

Dad was also a very intelligent student. He graduated from high school with honors when he was only 15 years old. That's a remarkable feat for any student during any era. Many recognized his mental acumen.

But what may have made Dad stand out the most was his musical giftedness. He possessed a moving, deep, resonant baritone voice. It thrilled all who heard him sing. As an adult, he was constantly invited to sing at weddings, funerals, special oratorios, and musical events all around the state of North Carolina. He even led different choirs during summer camps.

One of his most famous students in a summer choir was a young man named Andy Griffith. Years later, when Dad was pastoring a church in Kansas City, Andy Griffith was a part of a Broadway play that had come to town. Dad got tickets. After the show, he sent a card backstage to Andy and wrote a note on it. Within minutes, Dad was ushered into Andy's presence in his dressing room. Two old friends warmly greeted one another. They spent the evening together, talking and reminiscing about old times, Andy profusely thanking my dad for what he taught him about music and how to sing better.

My brother Howard inherited Dad's musical and voice gifts. He was a chip off the old block. When he sang, I couldn't tell the difference between Dad and him. Dad claimed continually that Howard was better than he was. If he was, it wasn't by much!

Again, both Dad and Mom's developmental years took place right in the middle of the Great Depression. So they and their families learned to get by on very little. It didn't take much for them to be happy. They possessed a deep faith in God. They cared for and supported one another in their respective families. They never realized they didn't have much. They had each other. Life was challenging, but they faced it together. As a result, they felt they could face most anything that came their way in life with the same faith and mental toughness they learned in their families.

Though they lived in the same city, Mom and Dad didn't know each other until they met on a double date. No, they weren't dating each other. I don't remember the name of Mom's date. In fact, I'm not sure she ever mentioned his name to us.

But Mom did often let us three kids know that Dad's date was named Evelyn. Whenever she got the chance, she threw a playful verbal jab at Dad about Evelyn. We loved it when she did so. We picked up on the frivolity and would also tease Dad about Evelyn.

He received all the teasing with a good-natured attitude. But he would also remind Mom that if it hadn't been for Evelyn and the infamous double date, they would have never met. Then he would laugh and say to us, "Nor would any of you be here." We all ended by saying, "Thank God for Evelyn!"

Mom and Dad started dating each other immediately after the double date. They didn't stop dating for the next 68 years. It was a torrid love affair. Almost from day one, they knew they wanted to get married.

There was one huge problem. Years before they met, Dad felt a call into the ministry. He knew that he needed to attend college and seminary. That was a seven-year commitment to do what was necessary to attain his sense of call from God.

His plan was to attend Moravian College and Seminary in Bethlehem, Pennsylvania, a whopping trip of hundreds of miles from Winston-Salem, North Carolina. Compounding the distance problem was a dreadful rule that a collegian and seminarian preparing for ministry could not be married until after graduation from seminary. That meant long years of waiting.

Mom and Dad became engaged and committed themselves to making the best of a complex and hard situation. Mom enrolled at Salem College in Winston-Salem. She worked toward a degree in elementary education. But what she really wanted was to be Dad's wife and eventually become a mother and support him in ministry.

During their long engagement, as often as possible, they would commute back and forth to see one another. There was no easy way to get from Winston-Salem to Bethlehem and vice versa. Long car, bus, and train rides were regularly experienced by both of them.

Long letters were penned between them. They were elaborately and affectionately written, especially from Mom to Dad. They yearned to be together. But they had to wait, year after year, until they could commit to becoming one.

They were steadfast about sharing the personal discipline necessary in this time of waiting—especially when they were together. Dad used to tell me that it was during this time period that they learned how to become best friends. They learned how to take advantage of every single second together.

After this long, arduous time of waiting, they were finally married in the early 1940s. Before God, their closest friends, and their family members, they expressed their eternal vows to one another so they could begin the process of becoming one flesh.

As like most in their day, they took their vows very seriously. It was a part of their family's heritage and supported by the moral consensus of the community in which they lived. As committed followers of Jesus, they promised to remain married forever. It was a permanent vow, for better or worse, whether rich or poor, in sickness or in health, forsaking all others, as long as they lived on earth. Divorce simply wasn't an option. The back door was locked from the outside.

They wanted a family, and kids started to arrive. First came my brother Howard. Three years later, my sister Carolyn was born. Finally, three years later, I arrived on the scene. Their family was complete.

Over a period of several decades, Dad's calls in ministry took him from Greensboro, North Carolina to Winston-Salem, North Carolina to Charlotte to Kansas City, Missouri to Orlando, Florida and then back to Charlotte for his final years of service.

As previously mentioned, Dad was extremely gifted musically. While serving a church in Winston-Salem, a talent agent from New York City heard him sing. He was convinced Dad could make it big on Broadway. He approached Dad and offered him a contract that would pay him ten times what he was making in ministry. He told Dad that he could make it big in the secular world.

Dad talked and prayed with Mom. Eventually, he turned down the offer. He felt called to be a minister of the gospel of Jesus Christ. He also knew that he could never be the husband and dad he wanted to be to us if he accepted the job. It would demand too much travel. He wanted to honor Mom. He turned it down. He never regretted this decision.

Mom faithfully followed Dad wherever he went. She felt his call was her call. For her, the most difficult move was when they left North Carolina to go to Missouri. She was a Tar Heel born and bred. She never dreamed she'd leave the state of North Carolina. I remember vividly seeing tears flow down her cheeks as we crossed the North Carolina border into Tennessee toward our new home in Missouri. But she was committed to going where Dad was called to go.

One specific time I remember Dad having honored Mom took place while we lived in Missouri. They really loved the church and the people. The church was growing and attracting new individuals and families.

We had been there for only three years when Mom developed a strange allergy to cold. When her body came in contact with something cold, she would swell up. No one could explain it. But it was dangerous—especially in the cold winter climate that was normal for Kansas City.

Doctors told Dad he should seek a church in a warmer climate. This was difficult to hear. Calls to a new ministry didn't normally come after having been in one place for only three years. But the allergy and its diagnosis were real. They were perplexed about what to do.

One of Dad's closest friends in the church was Roe Bartle, the mayor of Kansas City. He was a rotund man with a booming voice, a grand intelligence, and a larger-than-life personality. He was aware of Dad's conundrum and committed to praying with him for a solution.

One day, out of the blue, Mayor Bartle received a call from a large church asking if there would be any way Dad would be open to a call to become their pastor. They knew of their friendship. They knew Dad was a gifted preacher and leader, and wondered if he'd consider their offer.

Mayor Bartle approached Dad and told him about the phone conversation. Dad asked where the church was located. With a wry smile, Mayor Bartle responded, "Orlando, Florida." God's perfect providence became clearly evident in all this.

Eventually, Dad became the senior pastor of the First Presbyterian Church in Orlando, Florida. He gave up all he enjoyed in Missouri to love, serve, and honor Mom. God's divine hand was apparent in this call, for it had undoubtedly protected her against much suffering and most assuredly saved her life.

Dad and Mom ministered faithfully for 16 years in Orlando. Eventually they returned to Charlotte, where Dad oversaw the formation of a fledgling missions organization called the Outreach Foundation. He helped raise millions of dollars for overseas missions endeavors. He said these years were the most fulfilling of his ministry.

After the Outreach Foundation, Dad took interim calls at different churches. When a pastor would leave for another church, he would serve as an interim pastor who acted as a bridge between the departed pastor and the next one. Mom and Dad moved to several different places all over the southeast—staying anywhere between six months to two years in each location.

One interim ministry they especially enjoyed was the one at the First Presbyterian Church, Winston-Salem, North Carolina. It was like going home for them. They both still had family and friends living in the city. It was idyllic.

That is, until that dreadful day when Mom forgot to turn off one of the burners on the stove and almost caused a fire. That wasn't like her. She was the consummate cook. She was as adept in the kitchen as Russell Wilson is on the football field. She was an expert in all things culinary.

At the time, no one thought much of this mistake, especially Dad. As people age, we all have a few "senior moments," times when we forget something or another. That's only normal, right?

Then it happened again...and again...and again. Almost imperceptible memory lapses occurred with greater and greater frequency. They became increasingly vicious and cruel as well.

One event especially let us know what we suspected was happening. One mid-afternoon, Mom wandered from the house alone with no one knowing where she was. Dad became frantic and panicked. Several hours went by. Finally, a neighbor called to say he'd seen her several blocks away. When we went to get her, she didn't even remember having wandered away.

Soon thereafter, our worst fears were confirmed. Doctors diagnosed her with an advancing, slow-moving form of dementia. Most Alzheimer's patients experience memory loss and eventual death over an eight-to-nine-year life span. Mom's lasted for seventeen long, arduous years. We watched this gracious, kind, charming, loving woman slowly slip away and lose her mind. We watched Dad slowly lose his best friend.

My parents eventually had to sell their home and move into a facility where their needs could be better met. Dad was healthy and mobile. Mom was increasingly not.

By God's grace, they were able to spend some time together in a condominium in a retirement community. They were still able to have many lucid conversations and travel together. But the dark, foreboding shadow of dementia persistently hovered over their heads.

Mom progressively worsened to the point where she needed to move into an assisted living unit. Over time, her memory became so diminished that Dad had to move her into the Alzheimer's unit. No one wanted to place her there, especially Dad. But it was his only choice. She needed round-the-clock care.

It became very sad to go visit her. She would mindlessly sit in a chair, or her bed, most often with the television blaring in the background. She'd incessantly pick at her sweater, pulling at its threads. She didn't speak. At times, a smile might cross her face. Perhaps she recognized your face? But you weren't sure. Her eyes increasingly possessed a vacuous, haunting stare. You just didn't know if anyone was at home in her mind.

At this stage, the only time we ever got a response from her was when we sang some of her favorite old hymns. Amazingly, she would start singing them with us—word for word. Her faith that had sustained her since childhood still had a home in her heart.

Dad and Mom were experiencing what someone once called "the long good-bye."

Yet faithfully Dad visited her almost every single day. He would sit with her for hours, talking to her, sharing special memories, and singing songs to her, including the great hymns of the faith. Other times he would sing special love songs they had often sung as duets. Over and over again he would tell her he loved her.

Dad would stroke her hair and wipe her brow when it was wet with sweat. He would rub her back to keep the blood circulating. He would move her around so bedsores wouldn't develop. He would fetch water to wet her chapped lips, feed her food she was unable to bring to her lips, and somehow hope she knew he was present. Any time she gave him the slightest smile, his day was made.

It was sad to watch my dad see a part of himself die before his very eyes.

Once I asked Dad how hard it was to watch Mom die. "It's hard, son," he responded. But then he quickly added, "But I made a commitment to her. I promised for better or worse. This is worse. I promised in sickness and in health. This is sickness. I promised in richer or poorer. This is poorer. I made a promise 'till death do you part.' She is the love of my life. We are, after all, one flesh."

She died soon thereafter.

During her last years on earth, my dad especially honored my mom. She was his prized treasure. She was his permanent trophy bride. He exalted, valued, and esteemed her. For me, he was a living example of the definition of the word *honor*. His focus was on his beloved. I'll never forget that example.

Dad died with a hole in his heart some five years later. I once asked him if he'd ever consider remarrying. He recognized that some people experience the joy and privilege of having a new love in life after a spouse has died. But he knew this was not possible for him. He responded, "How could I ever marry again? I could never love another woman like I loved your mom."

She was his best friend for 68 years, and marriage partner for 63 of them. They shared most everything together. Their hearts and souls were interlinked as one.

When I think of the word *honor*, and ways for husbands to honor their wife, I think of my dad and his care for my mom. She was his prized treasure until she took her last breath—even when caring for her was extremely challenging.

My dad was an incredible example to me of how a husband can and should honor his wife. As Dad honored Mom, they truly became one— God's goal for all marriages.

I hope his example inspires you as well.

A Husband's Honor Code

On my honor, I will do my duty to my wife:

1. By trusting your gut. I will listen to, respect, and when needed, act upon your intuition when you deeply feel something for me.

2. By being a man of God. I will seek God's heart in all I do so you can trust and follow me when I try to lead us spiritually.

3. By encouraging your gifts. You are a uniquely gifted woman of God, and I deeply desire to see your gifts being maximized and launched into the world.

4. By respecting your opinion. I commit to spending time with you, empathizing with you, asking your opinion and listing the ways I can best honor you. I know you want only the best for me. I similarly want the best for you.

5. By asking you this question often: How is your heart? I sincerely care about what you are feeling. I definitely want you to tell me what's happening in your heart.

6. By sharing my heart with you. I commit to trying to get in touch with my own feelings and sharing them with you. I realize you are concerned about and want to know what's happening in my heart.

7. By being a guardian and gardener to you and our children. I will guard against all pernicious evils that seek to destroy us. I will add spiritual nutrients that will allow our family to grow spiritually.

8. By using my words wisely with you. I know that words can give life or death. Therefore, I want to use my words with you wisely in order to give you life, hope, and encouragement.

STUDY QUESTIONS

1

Trust Her Gut

Women's intuition can also be called gut instinct. In your own words, how would you define gut instinct?

Can you give one or two examples of times when your wife's intuition has sensed that there might be a potential problem of concern to you or your family? How did her intuition help you avoid a potentially painful problem?

Can you think of a time when you didn't listen to your wife's intuition, and she was correct? Can you identify why you didn't listen to her intuition? Have you been able to eliminate those reasons so you can better listen to her?

Read on pages 17-18 the four practical things you can do to give your wife an opportunity to share with you the concerns of her heart. List them here. Can you think of any additional things you can do?

2

Be a Man of God

This chapter lists four different character qualities women would love for their husbands to have. In the space after each item, (1) write a brief definition of the character quality, and (2) write an idea or two for how you can grow stronger in that quality.

Heroic Warrior—

Humble Worshiper—

A Forgiven Forgiver—

Bridled Power—

Which quality would you especially like to focus on in the days ahead, and why?

Can you put together two words that would describe the kind of man of God your wife would like for you to be? What would they be? What's keeping you from becoming this person?

3

Encourage Her Gifts

What are some of the ways your wife is gifted—including things she does better than anyone else? List them below. As you come up with answers, think of her skills, abilities, and anything she's good at doing.

Have you told your wife about the ways you think she is gifted? If so, what did you say? If not, why not?

What are some ways you've encouraged her gifts to be used?

As a husband, you are in the best position to encourage your wife in her areas of giftedness. With that in mind, answer these questions:

> How specifically can you be praying for her in the area of her gifts?

What doors can you help open so your wife can use her gifts more?

In what ways can you become your wife's biggest cheerleader?

Do you think she believes you support and encourage her giftedness?

Using your gifts together will help draw you closer. What common passions for ministry do you share together? In what ways are you serving together now? In what ways could you expand to new areas of serving together? Write your thoughts below, then take time to talk with your wife during an "alone time" this week! Plan together what that might look like.

4

Respect Her Opinion

The four ways to get to know your wife well are encapsulated in the acronym S-E-A-L.

S—*Study her life.* Your wife is a gift from God who can help you grow and succeed. In what ways have you benefited from her input? Would she say you know her well? What does she love to do? Love to do with you? What does she not like doing?

E—*Empathize with her.* Imagine being in your wife's shoes for a day. With that in mind, in what ways would you more diligently pray for her? In what ways would you show more appreciation for her? Through your empathy, how might you better serve her? Take time to tell her—today and always!

A—*Ask for her opinion.* When was the last time you've asked her opinion about a situation? In your family? Your job? In politics? Does she feel respected by you when she gives her opinions? Do you value her opinions?

L—*List what she says.* See the list on pages 68-69. Start writing your own list of things you have learned from your wife when she gives you input. Can you think of one or two right now? What are some things you do that she likes? What are some things you do that she doesn't like?

5

Ask This Question Often

The question every husband should ask his wife frequently is, "How is your heart?" But before you do this, what two things should you do?

—

—

Does your wife think you care about her heart? In what ways can you show that you really care about what's going on in her heart?

Can you readily identify "feeling" words? List the ones you use the most in your own speech.

How would your wife rate you as a listener? What can you do to improve in this area?

Set up a five-minute conversation with your wife. Then list all the feeling words she shares. Did you hear most of them?

What specific steps do you plan to take so that in the future, asking your wife the question "How is your heart?" becomes an ongoing habit?

6

Share Your Heart

We live in a culture that says men and husbands aren't supposed to share their hearts. What are the possible *negative* results of not sharing your heart?

What are the possible *positive* results of sharing your heart?

Reread on pages 97-98 what is said about the word *ezer* in relation to what a wife does. What are some ways your wife has been your *ezer*?

The goal of marriage is oneness. The more you share your heart, the more you and your wife can become one. What intentional steps can you take to share with your wife—sometime this week—the things that are weighing on your heart?

Has there ever been a time when you've made yourself vulnerable to your wife? How did she respond?

7

Be a Guardian and Gardener

Being a guardian and a gardener means being the spiritual leader of your home—protecting and serving your wife and children.

> Read Psalm 127:1. What would it look like to have the Lord build your house? That is, what can you do to make that happen?

> Again, read Psalm 127:1. What does a watchman do? How are you protecting your family from the enemy? Yourself from the enemy?

What personal weaknesses and vulnerabilities do you have that the enemy knows about? How are you protecting yourself against him?

As a gardener, you're to apply two spiritual nutrients to your family: God's Word and prayer.

> Read Deuteronomy 6:4-7, giving special attention to verse 7. What are some ways a dad can make God's Word an active part

of everyday life in the home? Which ones are you willing to commit to doing on a regular basis?

Are you aware of your wife's and children's needs, fears, or concerns? Make a list of what you need to pray God's Word over them.

What two or three Scripture verses can you pray over your wife and children right now that would help them? Take time to commit them to memory this week.

8

Use Words Wisely

Read 1 Peter 3:7, and its encouragement for you to live with your wife "in an understanding way." How do you rate yourself at doing this? Where do you see room for improvement?

Proverbs 18:21 says that life and death are in the tongue. Do your words to your wife give life or death? What would it look like for your words to give life?

On pages 134-142 are 11 different statements or ways you can speak in a way that honors your wife. Which two or three stood out to you the most? List them here, and explain why they stood out.

Chapter 8 already suggests 11 ways to use your words wisely. Can you think of one or two additional phrases or statements that would specially honor your wife amd warm her heart? What is your plan for saying them to her? Write them here.

As you finish this book, ask yourself: Do you honor your wife?
Would you call her your one-and-only prized, permanent trophy
wife? What one or two lessons in this book had the greatest impact
on you, and why?

Describe how you and your wife are one. What strategies do you have
for increasing your oneness?

Notes

1. "Jimmy Carter talks wife Rosalynn on their 69th anniversary," AOL.com, July 7, 2015, at http://www.aol.com/article/2015/07/07/jimmy-carter-talks-wife-rosalynn-on-their-69th -anniversary/21206264/.

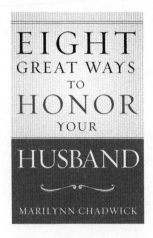

A wife is uniquely able to honor her husband in ways no one else can. In *Eight Great Ways to Honor Your Husband,* author Marilynn Chadwick shares how a wife can show this special kind of love:

become strong	guard your home
believe the best	lighten his load
build him up	dream big together
fight for him	create a culture of honor

When a wife honors her husband, both of them experience new heights of fulfillment and intimacy—and others will see how beautiful the husband-wife union can be when it follows God's design.

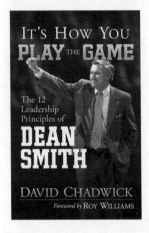

To learn more about Harvest House books and
to read sample chapters, visit our website:

www.harvesthousepublishers.com

HARVEST HOUSE PUBLISHERS
EUGENE, OREGON